Jesus said, "Feed my lambs."

JOHN 21:15

....

PRESENTED TO

....

BY

....

DATE

QUIET TIMES WITH GOD
published by Gold'n'Honey Books
a part of the Questar publishing family
© 1996 by Questar Publishers, Inc.
Illustrations © 1996 by xxxxx
Design by Kevin Keller
International Standard Book Number: 0-88070-964-2
Scripture quotations include selections from
The Holy Bible, New International Version
© 1973, 1984 by International Bible Society,
used by permission of Zondervan Publishing House
Printed in the United States of America

For information:
Questar Publishers, Inc.
Post Office Box 1720
Sisters, Oregon 97759

97 98 99 00 01 02 03 — 10 9 8 7 6 5 4 3 2

365 LITTLE DEVOTIONS

Quiet Times with God

by Mack Thomas

Illustrated by Terri Steiger

Gold 'n' Honey
BOOKS

Bright and Beautiful

The Bible says, "God's splendor is like the sunrise."
HABAKKUK 3:4

You've been awake early enough to see the sunrise, haven't you? Remember the beautiful colors you saw in the sky while the sun was slowly coming up?

On different days the sunrise has different colors. Sometimes we see lots of yellow, sometimes lots of pink, sometimes lots of orange, sometimes lots of red, and sometimes other colors, too.

A name we give to all those wonderful colors is the word splendor. God's sunrise is full of splendor — and so is God. He is bright, and He is beautiful.

So remember Him next time you see the sun coming up!

ENJOY READING PSALM 113:1-3

The Sun with Wings

The Bible says, "The sun of righteousness will rise with healing in its wings."
MALACHI 4:2

Oh, how warm the sun can feel! Can you remember a time when you felt the sun's heat on your face and all over? It's warm enough to make you feel good and strong.

Imagine this: The sun is like a great golden bird rising in the morning and flying across the sky. His shining wings are sending down light and warmth. And everyone who looks up to feel that warm light from those wings will become better and stronger.

The Bible says this is what the Lord is like. His light and warmth make us better and stronger. Look up to Him today!

READ TOGETHER HOSEA 6:3

More about Sunrises

The Bible says, "The rising sun will come to us from heaven."
LUKE 1:78

Not long before the baby Jesus was born, a man named Zechariah was praying to God. In his prayer he had a special name for Jesus. He called Jesus "the Rising Sun that will come to us from heaven."

Yes, Jesus came down to us from heaven above, like the sun that rises and shines down from the sky.

You can say a prayer like Zechariah did. You can pray this to God: "Thank You, God, for sending us Jesus from heaven, to shine on us today."

LOOK TOGETHER AT 2 CORINTHIANS 4:6

Our Crown

The Bible says, "The Lord Almighty will be a glorious crown."
ISAIAH 28:5

Crowns are worn by kings and queens and by every prince and princess. They hold their heads high, and they wear their crowns gladly. When we belong to God's family, we too can wear a crown — because every daughter of God is a princess, and every son of God is a prince.

And what is our crown? God is! Just knowing that God is our loving Father is like wearing a glorious crown! So don't forget His love and His care for you. Hold your head high, and be glad. You are a prince or a princess, and God Himself is your Father and your King.

ENJOY READING ISAIAH 51:11

The Best Crown

The Bible says, "We see Jesus...now crowned with glory and honor."
HEBREWS 2:9

Before Jesus was killed on a cross, His enemies put a crown of thorns on His head. The thorns were sharp. They hurt Jesus by cutting into His head. That was an awful time.

But now Jesus is the great King, and no one can ever hurt Him again. He sits on a majestic throne in heaven, and He wears a glorious crown. He is the King of Kings forever and ever.

This very moment, you can tell Jesus "Thank You" for wearing the crown of thorns. And you can tell Him you are glad that He now wears a much better crown.

ENJOY READING REVELATION 19:11-16

The Crown of Life

Jesus says, "Be faithful…and I will give you the crown of life."
REVELATION 2:10

If we believe in Jesus and keep loving Him and don't forget Him, then Jesus says He has something special waiting for us in heaven. He calls it "the crown of life," because it is so alive! It has everything you could ever want in a crown, and more.

This crown is not like anything you have ever seen in this world. It cannot get bent or broken. It can never fade or look old. And it will always fit you perfectly.

Jesus knows you will truly love wearing it in heaven. You can even tell Him "Thank You" right now that He has this crown waiting for you.

LOOK AT JAMES 1:12

Our Daily Bread

Jesus says to pray this: "Give us each day our daily bread."
LUKE 11:3

How we love our bread — as well as all the other food that goes with it, right? Isn't it good that God our Father gives us the food we need to keep our bodies healthy and strong?

God has promised to give us this food. But He likes us to ask Him for it each day. He wants us to ask Him because it is good for us to ask Him. It is good and right for us to remember that our food comes from God.

So ask Him today for your daily food — and don't forget to thank Him when you see it!

READ TOGETHER MATTHEW 6:25-33

The Bread of Life

Jesus says, "I am the bread of life."
JOHN 6:35

Jesus is like the bread that fills you up at mealtime. He is like the good food you enjoy so much when you are truly very hungry.

Listen to what Jesus says: "The one who comes to Me will never be hungry." What does Jesus mean?

If we are hungry to be good, and to be clean inside, Jesus is the One who can take care of that hunger. If we are hungry to do what is right and to be what is right, Jesus will help us. If we are hungry to know God better, Jesus will make sure it happens.

LOOK TOGETHER AT JOHN 6:33-35

More about Bread

The Bible says, "Jesus took bread, gave thanks and broke it."
LUKE 22:19

One night Jesus was with His closest friends and helpers —
His twelve disciples. Jesus knew that the next day He would
be nailed to a cross. He would die on that cross. This was the
punishment for their sins and your sins and my sins. He took
our punishment for all the wrong things we have ever done.

So on this night with His disciples, Jesus picked up some
bread, and He broke it. He said
that this bread was like His body.
The bread was broken, and His
body would be broken by the
nails. Let's tell Him "Thank You"
for doing this for you and me.

READ 1 CORINTHIANS 11:23-24

Jesus at the Door

Jesus says, "I stand at the door and knock."
REVELATION 3:20

Jesus stands knocking at a door. And He makes this promise: "If anyone hears my voice and opens the door, I will come in to him, and we will eat together."

Where is that door? What is on the other side of it? You are! This door is the way to get inside you! It opens up into everything you feel and everything you think. Jesus wants to live there inside you, all the time. But only you can open your door and let Him in.

If you have not asked Jesus to come live inside you, you can pray and ask Him to do that right now.

LOOK AT REVELATION 3:8 & 3:20

God's Door

Jesus says, "Knock and the door will be opened to you."
MATTHEW 7:7

God has many treasures He wants to give to you and to me. Think of these wonderful gifts like this:

They are wrapped and waiting for us in God's huge house in heaven. All we need to do is to knock at the door of His house each time we want another of those gifts. Then God will gladly open the door, and place the perfect gift in our hands.

How do you knock on His door? You do that by praying to Him. So remember to talk with God in prayer each day.

READ AND ENJOY MATTHEW 7:7-8

At the Door

The Bible says, "Blessed is the one who listens daily at my door."
PROVERBS 8:34

The cover of our Bibles is much like a door. We can open a door, or keep it closed. We can also open up our Bible, or keep it closed.

The Bible is like a doorway to God. Every day we can open that door, and listen for God to speak to us from the Bible. His words will always be wise words. If we listen carefully, they will show us how to live. They will show us how to know that God is smiling at us. They will show us how to truly be happy.

Will you be sure and listen at God's doorway every day?

READ AND UNDERSTAND PROVERBS 8:32-36

God Made Ears

The Bible says, "Ears that hear — the Lord has made them."
PROVERBS 20:12

God gave us ears so we can hear. He gave us only one mouth but two ears, because we should listen much more than we talk. God wants us to listen to Him speak to us from the Bible. And He wants us to obey what we hear.

He also wants us to listen to our parents and to our teachers, and to obey what they tell us.

He also wants us to listen to our friends and neighbors when they need our help. We can help them in many ways. We must listen to them carefully, so we will know what is best to do.

LOOK TOGETHER AT PROVERBS 21:13

Ears to Hear

Jesus says, "He who has ears, let him hear."
MATTHEW 13:43

Can you wiggle your ears? Many people can, and many people cannot. But all of us can hear with our ears, unless our ears are sick. So Jesus says we should use ears to hear.

Even when everything seems perfectly quiet, we can still listen to something. Besides our ears on the outside, we also have "inside ears." Our inside ears can always listen to what we are thinking. We can always be whispering into our inside ears. Are you thinking about good things today? Are you listening to God with your inside ears? Ask God to help you do this.

READ AND UNDERSTAND MATTHEW 13:36-43

Happy Ears

Jesus says, "Blessed are your ears because they hear."
MATTHEW 13:16

This word "blessed" means "happy." Our "inside" ears will be happy when they hear good things from Jesus.

Jesus has so many good things to keep telling us. Listen! He tells us how much He loves us. He tells us that God is His Father and our Father, too. He tells us that God our Father is good, and that God our Father is great and strong.

He tells us we don't have to be afraid, and we don't have to worry. He tells us that He will be with us forever. So listen to all those things. Listen and remember, and your ears will be happy.

ENJOY READING PSALM 78:1-4

Home Together

The Bible says, "God sets the lonely in families."
PSALM 68:6

God does not want us to be lonely. That's one of the big reasons He put you in your family.

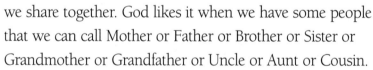

God likes to see us living with others in a home we share together. God likes it when we have some people that we can call Mother or Father or Brother or Sister or Grandmother or Grandfather or Uncle or Aunt or Cousin.

How many people can you call one of those names? Think of those people right now. Name them one by one. Thank God for giving them to you — and for giving you to them!

READ TOGETHER COLOSSIANS 3:20

Tell Your Family

Jesus says, "Go home to your family and tell them how much the Lord has done for you."
MARK 5:19

Once there was a man who was dirty, ugly, loud, and awful. Jesus found him living where dead people are buried. And Jesus made him clean and beautiful and quiet and good.

Then Jesus went on to help other people. This man wanted to go, too. But Jesus told the man instead to go home and tell his family how much God had helped him, though he didn't deserve it. So that's exactly what the man did.

What can you tell your family about what God has done for you? Think about it — and plan to say it before you open this book tomorrow.

READ THE STORY IN MARK 5:1-20

Your Bigger Family

*The Bible says, "Let us do good...especially to those
who belong to the family of believers."*
GALATIANS 6:10

God is so good! He not only gives us a family that we can live with in the same house. He also gives us a bigger family to be a part of.

This bigger family lives all around the world. Everyone who believes in Jesus and loves Him is a part of this family. Yes, this family is huge! It's called the family of God, and the family of believers.

God wants us to love everyone in His family. Can you name some other people who are part of this big family? What is something good that you can do for them?

TAKE A LOOK AT ROMANS 12:13

A House of Treasure

The Bible says, "The house of the righteous contains great treasure."
PROVERBS 15:6

This word "righteous" means people who know God and love Him. They do what God says is right. And in their houses are many great treasures.

What are these treasures? There is love for one another in that house. There are many smiles there. You can hear people pray in that house, and sing, and laugh. Everyone shares with each other there, and they help one another, and encourage one another.

But the best treasure there is this: God Himself lives in that house with them. What would you like to do to make sure your house is like this?

THINK ABOUT PROVERBS 24:3-4

More about Houses

A man in the Bible says this:
"I will walk in my house with blameless heart."
PSALM 101:2

The Bible hero named David is the man who wrote these words. He wrote them as a prayer to God. David decided that in his house, he would keep his heart "blameless." That means that at home David would always do what was loving and fair. As he walked from room to room he would think about how good God is, and he would praise God and thank God. This is what David decided to do.

Would you like to do this, too? If you would, say so to God in a prayer, just as David did.

TAKE A LOOK AT JOSHUA 24:15

Our Father's House

Jesus says, "In my Father's house are many rooms."
JOHN 14:2

God's heaven is like a house. Jesus says it's like a very big house with very many rooms. God is our Father there, and we will always be His children.

This house has always belonged to God, and it will always be His. But because He loves us, He wants to share it with us. Yes, you will always have a place to live. Even when you leave this world, you will have a place to call home! And God's home in heaven is bigger and better than any other place you have ever imagined.

READ AND ENJOY PSALM 23:6

A Lamp for the Path

A prayer in the Bible says this: "Your word is a lamp to my feet and a light for my path."
PSALM 119:105

In the old days (back in Bible times), lamps were much different from the lamps in your house. They were clay bowls filled with oil. A wick lying in the bowl would soak up the oil. It could be lighted like a candle wick. Those lamps did just what our lamps do today: They gave light.

The Bible is like that, too. It gives us light to live by. The Bible has God's words in it. The light of God's words can show us where to go, and what to do, and what to say. Every day you can turn on that light by listening to God's Word.

SEE GOD'S LIGHT IN PSALM 118:1

Let Your Light Shine

Jesus says, "People do not light a lamp and put it under a bowl."
MATTHEW 5:15

No, just as Jesus says, we don't light a lamp and then hide it. We put it where it will brighten up a whole room.

Jesus tells us to be like that. We should be like a lamp that shines on everyone in the room. And what is this light that can shine out from you and me?

Jesus says our light shines when we do what is good. People can see the good things we do, and hear the good things we say. When you are good to people, they will be glad. They will have such a good reason to tell God "Thank You."

SEE GOD'S LIGHT IN MATTHEW 5:14-16

Darkness into Light

*David prayed: "You, O Lord, keep my lamp burning;
my God turns my darkness into light."*
PSALM 18:28

Sometimes we just don't know what to do or what to say, or even what to think. It's like being in the dark.

That is always a good time to pray. We can ask God to give us light. We can ask Him to light a lamp for us and keep it burning. We can ask Him to show us what to do and what to say, and even what to think.

Light is better than darkness. God does not want us to stay in the dark. He always knows how to turn our darkness into light.

SEE GOD'S LIGHT IN JOHN 8:12

Jesus Holds the Keys

Jesus says, "I hold the keys of death and the grave."
REVELATION 1:18

In this world people die. When someone dies, the people who knew and loved that person are sad. We feel sad that this person has been taken away. It may seem like this person has been locked away from us. Who can unlock that lock, and let the person out?

Jesus can. Jesus holds the keys to death and to the place where dead people go. He always keeps the door of death unlocked for everyone who believes in Jesus and loves Him. They do not have to go and stay in the place of the dead. No, when they leave this earth, they go to be with Him. Today you can thank Him for this.

LISTEN TO JESUS IN REVELATION 1:18

Kingdom Keys

Jesus says, "I will give you the keys of the kingdom of heaven."
MATTHEW 16:19

Jesus spoke these words to His friends, the disciples. He promised to give them keys.

If you have keys, you can unlock doors and let people go in and out. The keys Jesus gave to His disciples could unlock the doors to heaven. What were these keys?

These keys were words. They were the words telling the story of Jesus. The disciples told this story to everyone they could, and they wrote it down in our Bible. Everyone who hears this story and believes in Jesus can now go through an unlocked door to heaven.

Tell Jesus "Thank You" today for opening up heaven's door to you.

LISTEN TO JESUS IN MATTHEW 16:19

A Key to Treasure

The Bible says, "The fear of the Lord is the key to this treasure."
ISAIAH 33:6

When God helps us, it is like finding a box full of treasure. When God teaches us and tells us His secrets, that is also like finding a treasure box.

How do we open this treasure? We can unlock it with a key that the Bible calls "the fear of the Lord." To fear the Lord means that we remember how awesome He is and how strong He is. We know how good He is, and we want Him to be pleased with us and not sad or angry. So we obey Him.

If you do what God tells you to do, you will find treasure.

ENJOY READING ISAIAH 33:5-6

God's Mirror

The Bible says, "Anyone who listens to the word but does not do what it says is like a man who looks at his face in a mirror..."
JAMES 1:23

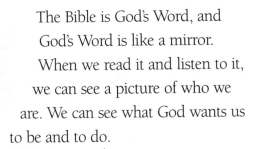

The Bible is God's Word, and God's Word is like a mirror. When we read it and listen to it, we can see a picture of who we are. We can see what God wants us to be and to do.

Be glad that you can listen to God's Word. Be very glad! But don't forget that we must do more than just hear God's Word. God wants us to do it. If we do not do what God says we should, it is just like turning away from the mirror and forgetting what we saw.

The next time you see a mirror, remember God's Word, and do it.

READ JAMES 1:22-25

Do Not Forget

The Bible says, "…like a man
who looks at his face in a mirror…"
JAMES 1:23

Have you heard God's Word? Have you listened to what He says in the Bible? Do you know what He wants you to do?

If you have, now is the time to do it. God always wants us to do what He tells us to do. He shows it to us. It is like looking in a mirror.

Please don't forget what God has told you. And the best way to not forget is to go ahead and do what He tells you to do.

Do now what you must do.

Remember to Do

The Bible says, "After looking at himself,
the man goes away and immediately forgets what he looks like."
JAMES 1:24

Do you know what you look like? Of course you do! You know because you have looked at yourself in a mirror, and you remember what you saw.

When we listen carefully to God's Word, we can see pictures in our mind and in our hearts. We see pictures of God and pictures of ourselves and pictures of other people. God wants us to remember these pictures. If we do what God tells us to do, we will not forget those pictures.

To keep on learning new things from God, remember to do what God tells you.

ONCE MORE, READ JAMES 1:22-25

Search Your Heart

The Bible says, "When you are on your beds,
search your hearts and be silent."

PSALM 4:4

When you are on your bed, with
nothing left to do except going
to sleep, here's something
else you can do: The Bible
calls it "searching your heart."
While you are quiet and still, you
can think about all that you did today.
Remember times when you were selfish
or rude, and tell God you were wrong. And remember that
Jesus died to take away your punishment for those sins.

Remember, too, all the things God showed you today, and
all the things He taught you. Be as quiet and as still as you
can, and search your heart.

ENJOY PSALM 4:8

Remembering in Bed

The Bible says, "On my bed I remember you;
I think of you through...the night."
PSALM 63:6

Late at night or early in the morning, when you are alone and quiet as you lie on your bed — remember that you are not really alone.

God is watching you, all the time. He knows everything you think and do and say when you're awake. And He knows every dream you dream when you are asleep.

God never goes to sleep, and He never gets tired. So if you wake up in the middle of the night, you can talk to Him. Think about Him, and pray to Him, there in the darkness. Call out to Him, for He always loves to hear your voice.

READ AND ENJOY PSALM 121:3-4

Singing in Bed

The Bible says, "Let the saints...sing for joy on their beds."
PSALM 149:5

When you are on your bed and not asleep, that is a good time to sing to the Lord.

Do you know some songs that praise God? Go ahead and sing them to the Lord with all your heart. (You may need to sing softly, so you don't wake up anyone else in the house.) You can also make up new songs to sing to Him. God especially likes this. Make up the words yourself, and sing them. Sing about how strong God is, and how loving God is.

Sing out to Him, for He loves to hear your voice.

READ AND THINK ABOUT PSALM 127:1-2

Your Inside Eyes

The Bible says, "Let us fix our eyes on Jesus…"
HEBREWS 12:2

You have two eyes that you can wink, blink, and see with.

You also have another set of eyes. They are inside you. The Bible calls them "the eyes of your heart" (in Ephesians 1:18). You can use these "inside eyes" to see what your two outside blinker eyes can never see. With these inside eyes you can see what God is like. With the eyes of your heart you can begin to see all the wonderful treasures we will have in heaven.

All by yourself, you can open up your outside eyes whenever you want. But only God can open your inside eyes. Ask Him to do that now.

READ CAREFULLY EPHESIANS 1:18-19

God Sees Everything

The Bible says, "The eyes of the Lord are everywhere..."
PROVERBS 15:3

God sees everything. God always sees everything you do and everything you think.

No one can ever hide from God. God can see through roofs and walls. He looks through mountains and oceans. He sees across the sky, beyond all the stars and the darkness. God is always keeping watch over all that He has made. He sees and knows everything that is happening.

So be glad, and praise God. Praise and thank Him for how great He is, that He can see everything.

READ AND THINK ABOUT HEBREWS 4:13

He'll Wipe Your Tears

The Bible says, "He will wipe every tear from their eyes."
REVELATION 21:4

When is the last time you had to wipe away your tears?

Did you know that someday God Himself will wipe away our tears? He has made a new heaven for everyone who believes in Jesus and loves Jesus. And in that new heaven He will live with us. He will be our God. He will wipe away our tears. No one there will die, and no one there will cry, and no one there will ever get hurt.

Yes, when that day comes you will see more than ever how good our God is and how great He is. And right now, today, you can tell Him "Thank You."

READ AND ENJOY REVELATION 21:1-4

Hairs Are Numbered

Jesus says, "Even the very hairs of your head
are all numbered. So don't be afraid..."
MATTHEW 10:30-31

Do you know how many hairs are on your head?

God does! He knows everything about you. He knows every little thing and every big thing about you, because He loves you so much. He knows every dream you dream at night. He knows every worry and every wish you think about in the daytime. He knows and hears your every prayer. He also knows your every fear. But He is strong and wise, and whatever you are afraid of, He can take care of it. Whenever any fear comes into your heart, tell God about it, and He can take it away.

Jesus says, "Don't be afraid."

TAKE A LOOK AT PSALM 56:3

A Forgiven Woman

*Jesus says, "She wet my feet with her tears
and wiped them with her hair."*
LUKE 7:44

Once there was a woman who had done many bad things
that were sad and ugly. She came to a house where Jesus had
been invited to eat dinner. The woman went into the house.
She had some sweet-smelling perfume with her. She found
Jesus, and got down beside His feet. She cried. She washed
His feet with her tears, dried them with her hair, and put the
perfume on His feet.

She loved Jesus so much, because
Jesus forgave her for so many bad and
ugly sins. She knew Jesus could save
her from her many sins.

Do you know this too?

READ THE STORY IN LUKE 7:36-50

A Beautiful Thing

*The Bible says, "Mary poured the perfume on Jesus' feet
and wiped his feet with her hair."*
JOHN 12:3

There was another time, too, when a woman used her hair to wipe the feet of Jesus. The woman's name was Mary.

Once again, Jesus was a guest for dinner at someone's house. Mary was also there. She had some perfume that cost a lot of money. Mary poured the perfume on Jesus' feet, and wiped them with her hair.

Jesus knew that He was going to die soon. He said that Mary was getting His body ready to be buried. Mary did a beautiful thing. And now, whenever people tell the story of Jesus, they also tell about what Mary did. What beautiful thing can you do for Jesus?

READ THE STORY IN JOHN 12:1-11

Humble in Heart

Jesus says, "I am gentle and humble in heart."
MATTHEW 11:29

Jesus is not proud and pushy. He is gentle and humble in heart. Jesus is never mean or rude. He is always gentle and humble in heart.

Jesus can teach us so much if we come to Him and learn from Him. Many times, what He teaches us is hard work. Sometimes it hurts a little. But even that hurt will make us feel better later. Jesus is a gentle teacher, and He is humble in heart. Jesus will do all He can to help you learn. He will stay beside you. He will never look down on you, or laugh at you.

So be glad, and praise Jesus, and tell Him "Thank You" for being gentle and humble in heart.

LISTEN TO JESUS IN MATTHEW 11:28-30

Pure in Heart

Jesus says, "Blessed are the pure in heart,
for they will see God."
MATTHEW 5:8

Jesus said that you will be very happy if you are clean inside.

If you are clean inside, you will be thinking about God, and about good things. You will not be thinking about bad things. You will not be worried. You will not be afraid. You will not be angry at anyone, or hating anyone. No, your heart will be clean.

Because your heart is clean, then the "inside eyes" of your heart will see God. And that is why you will be so happy.

LISTEN TO JESUS IN MATTHEW 5:1-10

All Your Heart

Jesus says, "Love the Lord your God with all your heart..."
MATTHEW 22:37

Jesus said that we should love God with everything that is inside us. Our heart should be as full of love for God as the ocean is full of water.

Do you know something about what you are like deep inside? Whatever you have deep inside you, that is what you should love God with. Love God with everything you are inside, and everything you have. Love God by thinking about Him, and talking to Him, and listening to Him.

What can you do right away to love God a little more with who you are inside? How can you love Him more before you open this book again tomorrow?

READ AND ENJOY MATTHEW 22:34-40

Stairway to Heaven

The Bible says, "Jacob had a dream in which he saw a stairway resting on the earth, with its top reaching to heaven..."
GENESIS 28:12

Are there any stairsteps in your house? If so, have you ever counted them all?

A man named Jacob once saw a stairway in a dream. But I'm sure he could never have counted those steps, because they went all the way up to heaven. Jacob had been walking alone on a long trip. One evening, when the sun went down, he lay down on the ground. He used a big stone for a pillow. He went to sleep, and dreamed. In his dream he saw the stairs going up to heaven. We can be glad that Jesus is like those stairs, because Jesus is our way up to heaven.

READ THE STORY IN GENESIS 28:10-15

A Promise for Jacob

The Bible says, "Jacob had a dream in which he saw a stairway...
and the angels of God were ascending and descending on it."
GENESIS 28:12

I'm sure Jacob never forgot this dream. He saw angels going up and down those stairs.

But there was even more to His dream. Above those stairs, Jacob saw the Lord. And Jacob heard the Lord speak. The Lord spoke a great promise to Jacob. The Lord promised to give him many children and a wonderful place to live. The Lord also promised to watch over Jacob, and to never leave him.

The Lord has also promised to watch over you, and to never leave you. Will you be as glad now as Jacob was?

READ AND UNDERSTAND HEBREWS 13:5-6

The Lord Is Here

The Bible says, "When Jacob awoke from his sleep,
he thought, Surely the Lord is in this place…"
GENESIS 28:16

When Jacob dreamed about the stairway to heaven, it helped him understand that God was very close to him.

Jacob awoke from his dream, and he said, "Surely the Lord is in this place, and I did not know it." Before his dream, Jacob thought He was alone. Now he knew that he was not.

You are never alone, either. God is always there. Sometimes we do not feel that God is nearby. We need Jesus to bring us closer to God. Jesus is our stairway to God. Jesus will help us to see and know how close God is.

READ THE STORY IN GENESIS 28:16-22

Daniel Prays

The Bible says, "Daniel went home to his upstairs room where the windows opened toward Jerusalem."
DANIEL 6:10

Do you have a window in your room?

In the Bible, Daniel had windows in his room. They opened toward Jerusalem, the city of God's people. Daniel could not see Jerusalem, because it was too far away. But he could look out his window and remember how much God loved His people. Three times a day Daniel prayed. He told God "Thank You."

The next time you look out a window, remember God. Right there beside the window, you can pray and tell God "Thank You" for something He has done for you.

READ AND ENJOY DANIEL 6

Falling Out a Window

The Bible says, "Seated in a window was a young man...
who was sinking into a deep sleep..."
ACTS 20:9

Once there was a young man who was sitting on a window sill. He was with some Christians. They were listening to their teacher, Paul. The young man was very tired. He went to sleep while Paul was teaching about God. Then the young man fell out the window!

Everyone hurried downstairs and outside. The young man was dead. But Paul put his arms around him. The young man became alive again! Everyone was so glad.

God can help us even when we have a terrible accident. Tell God "Thank You" for keeping us alive.

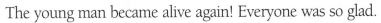

READ THE STORY IN ACTS 20:7-12

Through the Window

The Bible says, "Rahab let them down by a rope through the window…"
JOSHUA 2:15

Here is another Bible story about a window.

A woman named Rahab believed in God. But she lived in Jericho, a city where the people were God's enemies. When two of God's men came to Jericho, Rahab was good to them. She let them hide in her house, so God's enemies would not find them. When it was time for the men to go, she used a rope and lowered them out through a window in her house. The two men escaped from God's enemies.

Rahab was brave. The next time you see a window, remember how brave Rahab was for God.

READ THE STORY IN JOSHUA 2:1-15

Rebuilding the Walls

In the Bible, Nehemiah says, "Come,
let us rebuild the wall of Jerusalem."
NEHEMIAH 2:17

In the old days of Bible times, cities had stone walls around them. The walls were there to guard the people. The walls kept out their enemies.

Jerusalem was the city of God's chosen people. But when God's people disobeyed Him, He allowed an enemy to tear down the city walls. God did this to punish His people. When the punishment was over, God sent the man Nehemiah to help the people build back Jerusalem's walls. Nehemiah worked hard, and the people worked hard, and they built it quickly.

What work does God want you to do soon? Can you work hard, as Nehemiah did?

READ NEHEMIAH 4:6 AND 6:15-16

Walls Broken Down

The Bible says, "Like a city whose walls are broken down
is a man who lacks self-control."

PROVERBS 25:28

In the old days, when a city's walls were broken down, an enemy could come in to steal and to hurt.

Sometimes we can be like a city with broken-down walls. The Bible says we are like that when we do not have self-control. Self-control means you guard yourself. You say No to the things you should say No to. You do not let yourself do what you know is wrong.

If you do not have self-control, your enemy the devil can come in to steal and to hurt the good things inside you. Ask God now in prayer to help you be strong. Ask Him to give you self-control.

THINK ABOUT GALATIANS 5:22-23

Bright New Walls

The Bible says, "The city had a great, high wall…"
REVELATION 21:12

Someday there will be a bright new city of God, a New Jerusalem, a city coming down out of heaven from God. Everything there will always be sparkling and new.

God will always live with us there. We will see Him there and know Him. No enemy will ever get inside the city to hurt anyone. The city will have wonderful walls around it. These walls will be taller and thicker than any walls you have ever seen. They will shine with many colors, and all their light will come from God. The walls will be bright, just as God is bright. And they will be pure and clean, just as God is holy and pure and clean.

So be glad, and praise God for this city.

READ AND ENJOY REVELATION 21:10-12

Angel Wheels

The Bible says, "The spirit of the living creatures was in the wheels."
EZEKIEL 1:20

From where you are now, can you see any wheels? How many can you see?

God once opened up heaven and let a man named Ezekiel look inside. Ezekiel saw fire and lightning there. He also saw wheels. These wheels were not like any you or I have ever seen. All the wheels were next to four living creatures who were like angels. When the angels moved, the wheels also moved. The wheels sparkled and made noises.

Yes, in heaven there is lots of sound and light and motion. The next time you see a wheel, remember the sparkling wheels that Ezekiel saw. And give thanks to God that His heaven is so alive and interesting.

READ EZEKIEL 1:15-21

Throne Wheels

The Bible says, "His throne was flaming with fire,
and its wheels were all ablaze."

DANIEL 7:9

Just as Ezekiel did, a man named Daniel also got to look into heaven, and he saw some wheels.

The wheels Daniel saw were connected to a throne. The throne was the place where God Himself was seated. The throne was on fire. and the wheels were on fire. A river of fire came out from the throne. The fire of God is moving fire, like fire on wheels. The fire of God will burn up everything that is wrong and bad.

Give thanks to God for the wheels of fire at His throne. Always remember the fire that moves all around Him.

READ DANIEL 7:9-10

Chariot Wheels

The Bible says, "He made the wheels of their chariots come off..."
EXODUS 14:25

God knows everything about wheels.

Once in the Bible, God's people were being chased by their enemies. Their enemies were Pharaoh and his Egyptian soldiers. God opened up the sea so His people could cross over to the other side. The Egyptian soldiers came right in after them. They were driving chariots pulled by horses. But God made the chariot wheels stop working. Now the Egyptian soldiers knew they were in trouble! Suddenly the water of the sea washed back over them. The soldiers and the horses drowned.

The next time you see a wheel, remember how much God does to save His people.

READ THE STORY IN EXODUS 14:21-31

God's Belt

God says, "For as a belt is bound around a man's waist,
so I bound the whole house of Israel…to me."
JEREMIAH 13:11

The people of Israel were the first people God chose.

God picked the people of Israel to be His very own people. They were the first people who could say, "We belong to God." God brought them close to Him, just as a man wraps a belt close around his waist. God's people were to stay with Him, and always be with Him.

Today, everyone who believes in Jesus and loves Jesus is a part of God's people. We are like a belt around God's waist. We are to stay with Him, and always be with Him.

READ 1 PETER 2:9-10

Jesus' Belt

*The Bible says about Jesus, "Righteousness will be his belt
and faithfulness the sash around his waist."*
ISAIAH 11:5

These words about Jesus were written down by a man
named Isaiah. Isaiah wrote them long, long ago. Many years
before Jesus was born in Bethlehem, God showed Isaiah
what Jesus would be like. So Isaiah wrote down what God
showed him. And we can still read those words,
and enjoy them.

God showed Isaiah that Jesus would be
righteous. Righteous means doing what is
right. Jesus always does what is right.
Righteousness is always with Him, like a
belt around His waist.

Right now, you can tell Jesus "Thank You"
that He is always righteous.

LOOK AT PSALM 119:137

Our Belt

The Bible says, "Stand firm then,
with the belt of truth buckled around your waist..."

EPHESIANS 6:14

We should always tell the truth. The truth should always be with us. It should be like a belt around our waist that we never take off. God wants it that way. God wants all His children to always tell the truth.

If we do not tell lies, then we will be stronger. We can stand up and be strong like soldiers for God.

Have you told someone a lie? If you have, then you can go back to that person now and tell the truth. You can say you were wrong to tell that lie.

Always tell the truth.

READ CAREFULLY COLOSSIANS 3:9-10

A Place for Your Best

The Bible says, "Noah built an altar to the Lord…"
GENESIS 8:20

In the old days of Bible times, men made altars. The altars were usually made from stones. They were places where God's people could give things to God. They gave God the best food they had, and the best animals they had. They put these good things on the altar. They gave their best to God.

You can also give your best to God. When you remember to tell God "Thank You" for what He has given you, that is a good gift to God. When you do your best to help someone, and to share everything you have, that is also a good gift to God.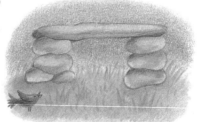

What can you give to God?

LOOK AT EXODUS 20:24

A Better Altar

The Bible says, "We have an altar…"
HEBREWS 13:10

Many, many altars were built by the heroes of Bible times. Noah built an altar after he left the ark. Abraham built altars in the places where God talked to him. Jacob built an altar where he dreamed about the stairway to heaven. Solomon made an altar of gold for the temple. Isaac, Moses, Joshua, Gideon, David, and Elijah all built altars.

But we have a much better altar than any of those. Our altar is in heaven. It is where God always remembers how His Son Jesus Christ died for you and me.

So be glad, and tell God "Thank You" for this altar.

READ HEBREWS 13:10-13

First Do This

Jesus says, "Leave your gift there in front of the altar.
First go and be reconciled to your brother."
MATTHEW 5:24

An altar can be any place where you take time to pray to God.

An altar can be any place where you tell God that you belong to Him, and that your room and your toys and your clothes and your money and everything you have belongs to Him.

But suppose you are telling God this — and suddenly you remember that your brother or sister is angry with you. Then go at once to your brother and sister, and tell the truth. Say that you are sorry for what you did, and that you want to be friends.

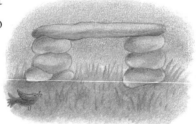

LISTEN TO JESUS IN MATTHEW 5:23-24

Voice from a Cloud

The Bible says, "A voice from the cloud said,
This is my Son, whom I love…"
MATTHEW 17:5

Have you seen any clouds in the sky today? If so, were they bright and white, or dark and gray?

Once a bright cloud came down on a mountain where Jesus was pray-ing. It was brighter than any cloud you and I have ever seen. Jesus was on the mountain with three of His friends. While they were there, Jesus' face became as bright as the sun. His clothes became as bright as snow. Then God's voice sounded from the cloud. God said that Jesus is His Son. God said He loves Jesus. And God said, "Listen to Him!" God wants us to listen carefully to everything Jesus says.

READ THE STORY IN MATTHEW 17:1-8

Up into the Clouds

*The Bible says, "We will be caught up…in the clouds
to meet the Lord in the air."*
1 THESSALONIANS 4:17

Someday you and I will go up into the clouds. But we will not be in an airplane or helicopter. No, God Himself will bring us up into the air.

Everyone who believes in Jesus will go up into the clouds together to meet Him there. He has promised us that this will happen. When will it happen? We don't know! It could be before you go to sleep tonight. Or it could be after you are grown up. But we know for sure that it will happen someday, because God has promised.

So — if it happens even before you close this book — are you ready?

READ 1 THESSALONIANS 4:15-18

Coming with Clouds

*The Bible says, "Look, he is coming with the clouds,
and every eye will see him…"*
REVELATION 1:7

The Bible tells us to always be ready and watching for Jesus to come back.

Someday soon we will see Him up there in the clouds. Someday soon we will say to each other, "Look! I see Him!" And from all around us we will hear others answer, "Yes! I see Him too!" When we see Him we will all know for sure that it is Jesus.

People who will not love Jesus will be terribly afraid when they see Him, because He will punish them. But we will be glad, because we believe in Him and love Him.

READ REVELATION 1:7-8

Highway of Holiness

God says, "A highway will be there;
it will be called the Way of Holiness."

ISAIAH 35:8

There is a road that is only for people who believe in Jesus, and love Him. It is a good road, and a smooth highway. The Bible calls it the Way of Holiness.

We will always be safe as we walk along that road. No wild animal can attack us there. Everyone who goes on that road will sing and be glad. The farther we go, the happier we will be, and the more we will sing.

This road will take us to the City of God and His people. When we get there, we will be more glad than we have ever been.

ENJOY READING ISAIAH 35:8-10

Road to Emmaus

The Bible says, "They asked each other, Were not our hearts burning within us while he talked with us on the road?"
L U K E   2 4 : 3 2

Two men were once walking on a road. They were going from Jerusalem to a small town called Emmaus. They were sad.

Another Man came up behind them. He began walking and talking with them. He knew all the words in the Bible. He talked about those words. He explained how these words were all about Jesus. Now the first two men were not sad anymore. They were glad and excited. When they reached Emmaus, they all went inside a house. Suddenly the first two men found out who the other Man was. It was Jesus Himself!

Are you excited when you hear what the Bible says about Jesus?

READ THE STORY IN LUKE 24:13-35

The Narrow Road

Jesus says, "Narrow is the road that leads to life."
MATTHEW 7:13

Jesus is walking down a road, and He wants us to walk with Him. But the road is not wide. And the road is not easy. Rocks could crash down from the steep hills nearby. Or we might slip and fall into the deep ditch running beside us.

So why should we take such a dangerous road? The first reason is that this road leads to life! It takes us to everything that is truly good and alive.

The second reason (and the best) is that Jesus Himself will be with us all the way. And we want to go where Jesus goes.

ENJOY READING MATTHEW 7:12-14

Lamb of God

The Bible says, "Look, the Lamb of God!"
JOHN 1:29

Some people were together beside a river. And Jesus was walking toward them. So a man named John got everyone's attention. He pointed to Jesus and said, "Look! The Lamb of God who takes away the sin of the world!"

Why did John call Jesus the Lamb of God? You have seen a lamb, haven't you? A lamb is not mean or wild. A lamb is gentle and quiet.

Jesus is not mean or wild either. He is so gentle with us. He speaks quietly to us. And He takes away our sins — the wrong things and the bad things that we have done.

LOOK TOGETHER AT JOHN 1:28-34

The Best Lamb

*The Bible says, "…the precious blood of Christ,
a lamb without blemish or defect."*
1 PETER 1:19

In the old days of Bible times, people
would give their best lambs to God.
Nothing could be wrong with the
lambs. They could not be bad or
ugly. The lambs would be killed
with a knife, and they would bleed.

This showed God's people some-
thing very important. God cannot forgive our sins unless
Someone bleeds and dies.

Jesus is the Lamb who bled and died for us. Nothing was
ever wrong with Jesus. And He never sinned. So He was the
Lamb who bled and died for you and me. Be glad, and tell
Jesus "Thank You" for dying to take away your sins.

READ TOGETHER 1 PETER 1:18-21

The Lamb's Supper

*The Bible says, "Blessed are those who are invited
to the wedding supper of the Lamb!"*
REVELATION 19:9

Jesus is the Lamb of God. Someday we will see the Lamb of God, and know Him. We will be with the Lamb of God in heaven. The Lamb will be like a lamp in the city. Jesus will give us light. Everyone there will sing to the Lamb. We will bow down before Him, and praise Him. He will seem so wonderful and good to us that we will never stop saying good things about Him. We will have a huge dinner with Jesus. It will be like a party, and everyone will be glad to be there.

Right now, tell Jesus "Thank You" that He has invited you to His wonderful party.

ENJOY READING REVELATION 19:6-9

Fingers for Battle

*The Bible says, "Praise be to the Lord...
who trains my...fingers for battle."*
PSALM 144:1

David praised God, because God showed him how to be a good soldier. God taught David's fingers to use the sword and the spear and the bow and arrow. David became the leader of God's soldiers as they went into battle against God's enemies.

God will also train your fingers to do the work He has for you.

So be glad, and praise God. Praise and thank Him that He will teach you everything you need to know, to do the work He gives you.

READ TOGETHER PSALM 18:32-34

Fingers at Work

The Bible says, "Jesus put his fingers into the man's ears."
MARK 7:33

One day some people brought a man to Jesus. The man could not hear anything. And when he talked, people could not understand him.

His friends begged Jesus to touch this man. So Jesus took him away by himself. Jesus showed the man what He would do. He put His fingers in the man's ears. He also touched the man's tongue. Then Jesus looked up to God. He said, "Be opened." Suddenly the man could hear everything. When he talked, everyone could now understand him.

So be glad, and praise Jesus, because He does everything so well.

READ THE STORY IN MARK 7:31-37

Writing in the Dirt

The Bible says, "Jesus bent down
and started to write on the ground with his finger."
JOHN 8:6

Have you ever used your finger to draw pictures or letters in the dirt?

Jesus did this one day. Some men came to Jesus. They brought with them a woman who had done something wrong. They wanted to throw rocks at her. Jesus knew these men were being bad. So He talked to them. Then He bent down to write in the dirt. When He looked back up, all those bad men were gone. Then Jesus looked at the woman, and told her to stop doing those wrong things.

The next time you write with your finger in the dirt, remember how good Jesus is to everyone.

READ THE STORY IN JOHN 8:1-11

Every Knee Will Bow

The Bible says, "…that at the name of Jesus
every knee should bow…"
PHILIPPIANS 2:10

In the old days people often got down on their knees when they saw someone who was their king or leader. This was their way of showing that this person was strong, and could do with them whatever he wanted.

There are many people today who will not say that Jesus is their King and their Leader and their Lord. They do not want to believe that He can do with them whatever He wants. But someday they will have to admit who Jesus is. They will have to get down on their knees and say that Jesus is Lord, whether they like it or not.

But you and I are glad that Jesus is our King and our Lord. So let's gladly be on our knees to tell Him!

READ AND REMEMBER PHILIPPIANS 2:8-11

On Our Knees

The Bible says, "Peter got down on his knees and prayed."
ACTS 9:40

One of the reasons God gave us knees is so we could get down on them sometimes when we pray. This is a good way for us to show that He is our King and our Lord and our Leader. This is a good way to tell Him that He can do with us whatever He wants.

When we bow down on our knees we can tell God that He is so much bigger and better than we are.

So whenever you want to get on your knees to show God these things, go ahead and do it. Be glad to be on your knees before your King and your Lord.

READ AND ENJOY PSALM 95:6-7

Jesus Wants To

*The Bible says, " A man with leprosy came to him
and begged him on his knees…"
Mark 1:40*

One day a sick man came to Jesus. He
had leprosy. This awful disease made his
skin ugly, and no one ever wanted to touch
him. They thought he was terribly dirty.
Right in front of Jesus, this man fell
down on his knees. He knew Jesus was
better than He was. He knew Jesus could do with
him whatever He wanted. He said to Jesus, "If You want to,
You can make me well." Jesus reached out and touched the
sick man. Jesus said, "I do want to. Be well!" At once the
man's ugly disease went away.

So be glad, and praise and thank Jesus that He can
do this.

READ THE STORY IN MARK 1:40-42

Palm Trees

The Bible says, "On the walls all around the temple…
he carved cherubim, palm trees and open flowers."

1 KINGS 6:29

In the Bible, God's people built a beautiful building where they could come to Him. It was called the temple.

God told David how to build it. David told Solomon. Then Solomon built the temple in Jerusalem. The walls inside the temple were decorated with pictures. There were pictures of angels and flowers and palm trees. These were the most beautiful trees in the land where God's people lived.

The temple was made to be beautiful, because God is beautiful. When you see something beautiful, remember how beautiful God is, and how much He likes beautiful things.

READ 1 KINGS 6:29-32

Palm Branches

The Bible says, "They took palm branches
and went out to meet him…"
JOHN 12:13

One day Jesus came into Jerusalem. He was riding on a donkey.

The people in Jerusalem were so glad to see Him. They took off their coats, and threw them down in front of Jesus. It was like putting a carpet on the road for Jesus to ride over. They also waved beautiful palm branches in the air. They shouted their praise to Jesus. They said, "Hosanna! How good and happy is our King, who comes in the name of the Lord!"

They waved those palm branches because they were happy. What can you do today to show how glad you are that you belong to Jesus?

READ THE STORY IN JOHN 12:12-15

Heaven's Palm Branch

In the Bible, John says, "There before me was a great multitude…
holding palm branches in their hands."
REVELATION 7:9

A day is coming in heaven when a great crowd of people will gather around the throne of God. They will come from everywhere in the world.

Palm branches will be in their hands, so they can wave them high. And they will shout praises to God, and to Jesus the Lamb of God. They will praise God because they are glad that Jesus has saved them from their sins.

Imagine that you are there stretching your hands high, and swinging palm branch back and forth. And you shout, "Thanks God, for saving me!" Can you tell Him those words in a prayer today?

READ AND ENJOY REVELATION 7:9-12

Small Seeds

Jesus says, "If you have faith as small as a mustard seed…
nothing will be impossible for you."
MATTHEW 17:20

Have you ever held some seeds in your hand? Seeds are not very big, are they?

Jesus says that our faith is like a seed. What is faith? Faith means believing. Faith means you know that God will do exactly what He says He will do. If you have faith, you really do believe what God says. You can do so many good things if you believe in Jesus even just a little — even if your faith is only as much as a little seed.

What good things does God want you to do very soon? Do you believe that God can help you do them? Remember to talk with God about this in a prayer.

LISTEN TO JESUS IN MATTHEW 17:14-20

The Seed Is the Word

Jesus says, "The seed is the word of God."
LUKE 8:1

Have you seen how seeds will grow? If you put a seed in the right kind of dirt, the seed will sprout up as a plant. The plant will grow healthy and tall. But the wrong kind of dirt is not good for the seed. If the soil has too  many rocks or weeds, the seed cannot become a tall, healthy plant.

Jesus said that God's words are like seeds. When you and I hear God's words, the seeds are planted inside us. If we are like good soil inside, God's words will grow into something good and big and healthy.

Your soil inside is good if you listen carefully to God's Word, and then do it.

LISTEN TO JESUS IN LUKE 8:4-15

When a Seed Dies

*Jesus says, "If a kernel of wheat falls to the ground
and dies...it produces many seeds."*
JOHN 12:24

A seed gets planted deep in the dirt. If the seed could talk it might say, Get me out of here! This is like dying and being buried! I'm all alone in this cold, dark ground!

But when a seed dies like this, it is for a good reason. Soon the seed can sprout up as a little plant. The plant can grow tall and healthy. And the grown-up plant can make many, many more seeds.

Jesus says we should be like that seed. So don't be selfish, like a seed that doesn't want to get planted. Tell God that you will let Him plant you anywhere He wants.

Wind and Spirit

Jesus says, "The wind blows wherever it pleases."
JOHN 3:8

Do you like to hear the wind blowing? Do you like to feel it on your face? Do you like to see it tossing the tree branches?

Jesus said the Holy Spirit is like the wind as He comes to live inside us. You cannot see Him as He does His work. You cannot see what He is going to do next. But you know when He is here.

God has sent His Holy Spirit to live inside everyone who believes in Jesus and loves Jesus. God's Holy Spirit comes to open up our "inside eyes." Then we can really start to see and understand what God is like. The next time you hear the wind, remember God's Holy Spirit.

LISTEN TO JESUS IN JOHN 3:5-8

Wind and Spirit

The Bible says, "Suddenly a sound like the blowing of a violent wind came from heaven and filled the whole house…"
ACTS 2:2

God's Holy Spirit is like the wind. And God's Holy Spirit is strong. When He comes to live inside us, He makes us strong as well.

One day Jesus' friends were all together in a house. Jesus was not with them. He had gone back up to heaven. Suddenly in that house, Jesus' friends heard a loud noise. It sounded like a very strong wind. It filled all that house.

That was the day the Holy Spirit came to live inside all of Jesus' friends who were there. They all became strong. They began to talk to everyone about Jesus and the great things God has done. So ask God's Holy Spirit to make you as strong as they were.

Wind and Spirit

The Bible says, "He brings out the wind from his storehouses."
PSALM 135:7

God is great. The Lord our God always does whatever He pleases.

The Lord our God is the Maker of the mighty wind that cleans the air. In the whole world, He knows where every breeze has come from, and where every breeze is going. Only God can make all these breezes blow. And only He knows all about them.

God's Holy Spirit is mighty like the wind. Ask God to use His Holy Spirit inside you. Ask Him to blow away any bad things inside you, and leave you clean.

READ AND ENJOY PSALM 135:5-7

Nailed to a Cross

In the Bible, Peter says, "And you, with the help of wicked men, put him to death by nailing him to the cross."
ACTS 2:23

Many people in Jerusalem were angry with Jesus. Jesus was telling them about the wrong things they were doing. They did not like this. They did not want to admit that Jesus is God and Lord. So they grabbed Jesus and beat Him. They tore off His clothes. They nailed His arms to a big wooden cross. They also nailed His legs to the cross.

Always remember how much this hurt Jesus. It hurt more than any hurt you or I have ever known. It hurt Him terribly, and it was ugly and mean and cruel and shameful.

Why did Jesus let them do this to Him? So he could die for you and me. So be glad, and tell Jesus "Thank You."

READ MARK 15:22-24

Nail Marks

*In the Bible, Thomas says, "Unless I see the nail marks
in his hands...I will not believe."*

JOHN 20:25

Jesus died. But three days
later He rose from the
dead. Yes, He was alive!

That night His friends
were together. Suddenly Jesus
was with them. But Jesus' friend Thomas was not there. The
other men kept telling Thomas later that they saw Jesus alive.
But Thomas would not believe it was Jesus. Thomas said he
needed to see the nail marks in Jesus first.

Soon Jesus came to His friends again. This time Thomas
was there. Jesus showed His nail marks to Thomas. This time
Thomas believed. Jesus says we will be happier if we believe
in Him even without seeing His nail marks.

READ THE STORY IN JOHN 20:19-29

Nailed to a Cross

The Bible says, "He took it away, nailing it to the cross."
COLOSSIANS 2:14

When Jesus was nailed to the cross, something else was nailed there too. We could not see it. But God knew it was there.

What was it? It was a long list written down. It was a long list of every time we did not obey one of God's rules.

When Jesus died, the Bible says this list was nailed to the cross with Jesus. This list died too. It was wiped away. It has disappeared, because now God forgives us. He forgives us because Jesus paid the punishment for our sins. So be glad, and tell Jesus "Thank You."

READ CAREFULLY COLOSSIANS 2:13-15

Carrying His Cross

The Bible says, "Carrying his own cross,
he went out to the place of the Skull."
JOHN 19:17

When soldiers took Jesus to be
killed, they made Him carry His cross.

If you had been on those streets
as Jesus walked by, you would see
Him bleeding. You would see Jesus
hurting. What would you think? What
would you say to Him?

Jesus never thought about stopping or trying to run away.
Jesus knew this was what God wanted Him to do. Jesus
could die and take away your sins and mine. Jesus loves us.
Jesus wants us to be in heaven with Him. And Jesus knew
that we could not be there unless He carried His cross and
died for our sins.

READ AND REMEMBER HEBREWS 12:2

Death on a Cross

*The Bible says, "He humbled himself and became obedient
to death—even death on a cross!"*
Philippians 2:8

Dying on a cross is ugly and cruel. But this is what God
wanted Jesus to do. Jesus obeyed His Father. He let soldiers
nail Him to the cross.

Two other men were killed on crosses that same day. Both
men had done many wrong things. They were being punished.
One man was mean to Jesus and mocked Him. But the man
on the other cross knew Jesus had done nothing
wrong. He said, "Jesus, remember me
when You come into Your kingdom."
Jesus answered, "Today you will be
with me in paradise."

Remember that Jesus is your King.
Jesus will always remember you.

READ THE STORY IN LUKE 23:32-43

Carrying Our Cross

*Jesus says, "Anyone who does not carry his cross
and follow me cannot be my disciple."*

L U K E   1 4 : 2 7

Jesus said many times that we must carry our cross and follow Him. What did Jesus mean?

When Jesus carried His cross, He was on His way to die. He was thinking about God and about all the people of the world, like you and me. He was not selfish. He was not thinking about Himself. He was not trying to have things easier for Himself.

When we carry our cross, it means we cannot be selfish. We think about God and about other people. We live for them, not for ourselves. If we want to live this way, God will help us. Do you want to live this way?

LISTEN TO JESUS IN LUKE 9:23

Let Birds Fly

God says, "Let birds fly above the earth
across the expanse of the sky."
GENESIS 1:20

God made the birds to fly so high.
Maybe you have wanted to fly
like a bird. And someday, like an
angel you will.

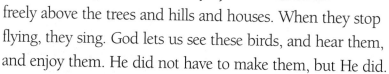

But for now, here on earth, we
can look up and watch the birds
with their wings out wide. They fly so
freely above the trees and hills and houses. When they stop
flying, they sing. God lets us see these birds, and hear them,
and enjoy them. He did not have to make them, but He did.

Tell God "Thank You" for making something so wonderful as the birds that fly and sing.

TAKE A LOOK AT GENESIS 1:20-23

Look at the Birds

Jesus says, "Look at the birds of the air."
MATTHEW 6:26

Jesus tells us to look at the birds flying in the air. As we do, Jesus tells us to think about them. He helps us remember that the birds do not plant any gardens or harvest any crops. They do not build any barns to store their food.

But God still feeds them. Jesus helps us remember that the God who feeds the birds is your heavenly Father, and mine, too. And you and I are much more important to God than the birds.

If God takes such good care of the birds, then He will most certainly take good care of you and me. So don't forget to tell Him "Thank You."

LISTEN TO JESUS IN MATTHEW 6:26

No Place to Rest

*Jesus says, "Birds of the air have nests,
but the Son of Man has no place to lay his head."*
LUKE 9:58

When Jesus was a boy, He lived with Mary and Joseph. But after He grew up, He left this home. He walked from place to place, all over the land of Israel. He went everywhere to teach people about God. When night came He would sleep wherever He was. One night He even slept in a boat. And at least once He did not sleep at all. Instead He stayed up all night and prayed to God.

The Man Jesus did not have a house. He did not even have a nest, like the birds do.

But now Jesus is at home with God in heaven. And He is making this our home, too.

LISTEN TO JESUS IN LUKE 9:57-62

The Grass Grows

The Bible says, "He makes grass grow…"
PSALM 104:14

God makes grass grow almost everywhere in the world. Many, many animals can eat the grass. God waters this grass with rain. The rain comes down from the clouds which God makes in the sky.

The next time you see grass, remember how God is kind and good. Remember that He watches over all the world, and takes good care of it. Remember all that He does to make the green grass grow.

So be glad, and praise God. Praise and thank Him that He takes such good care of all the world.

LOOK AT PSALM 147:8

Plenty of Grass

The Bible says, "There was plenty of grass in that place."
J O H N 6 : 1 0

One day Jesus was in a place where there was lots of good green grass. There were also many people with Jesus. He was helping and teaching the people. They were with Him for a long time.

Soon they became hungry. Now, good green grass is the right food for many animals, but not for people. The people there that day did not have much people food. They only had just a little bread and fish. Jesus asked all the people to sit down on the grass. Then He changed that little bit of food into lots of bread and lots of fish! Everyone had plenty to eat.

So be glad that Jesus can do such a miracle.

READ THE STORY IN MATTHEW 14:13-21

Like Grass

The Bible says, "All men are like grass…; the grass withers…"
1 P E T E R 1 : 2 4

Grass does not stay green forever. When there is no rain, or when cold weather comes, the grass turns brown and dies.

The Bible reminds us that this is what we are like in this world. Someday every man and woman in this world will die. We do not live here forever.

But because we believe in Jesus and love Him, we do not need to be afraid to die. When we leave this world, we will live with Jesus forever. God has promised this to us. So tell God "Thank You" that He always keeps His promises, and we will live with Him forever.

READ CAREFULLY 1 PETER 1:22-25

Marking the Seasons

The Bible says, "The moon marks off the seasons…"
PSALM 104:19

Some nights the moon is a round circle, big and full. Each night after that, part of the circle gets darker. Soon all the circle is dark. Then little by little more of the moon lights back up. Finally a night comes when the moon is again a round circle, big and full.

When the moon does all this three times, our cold winter has become spring. Three times more, and spring becomes warm summer. Three times more, and summer becomes fall. Three times more, and fall becomes another winter.

Give praise to God for the wonderful way He made the moon to shine and mark off our seasons.

READ GENESIS 1:14-19

The Moon Goes Dark

Jesus says, "In those days…the moon will not give its light…"
MARK 13:24

A night is coming when the moon should be shining, but it will not. The moon will become dark. It will be a terrible night for everyone who does not believe in Jesus or love Jesus. In that terrible time of darkness, God will punish the people who do not believe in Him and love Him.

God is so good. He does not want there to be anything bad anywhere. So the time is coming when He will throw away everything bad. He will punish everyone who will not let Jesus make them good.

Give thanks to God now that He is so good. Give thanks to Him that He will throw away everything bad.

LISTEN TO JESUS IN MATTHEW 24:29-51

No Moon

*The Bible says, "The city does not need the moon to shine on it,
for the glory of God gives it light…"*
REVELATION 21:23

Someday we will see our new home from God. It is the New Jerusalem, the city coming down out of heaven from God.

There we will never see the moon. We will not need the moon to mark our seasons, because there is no time there. No one will ever grow old. No one will ever be in a hurry.

We will not need a moon, because it will never be night there. We will never again see shadows or darkness. We will hear no strange noises at night. Nothing dark will ever make us afraid again. So give thanks to God for this bright home that we will have.

READ AND ENJOY REVELATION 21:22-27

He Sends the Rain

*The Bible says, "He supplies the earth with rain
and makes grass grow on the hills."*
P S A L M   1 4 7 : 8

Give thanks to God for the rain He sends!

If it did not rain, we would soon have no water to drink. If it did not rain, the plants in our gardens and the crops in the farmers' fields would not grow. We would soon have no food.

God makes the rain clouds as only He can. He makes every raindrop as only He can. Each one is cool and wet and wonderful, for God Himself made it. The next time you see or feel a cool and wet and wonderful raindrop, don't forget who made it!

READ AND ENJOY PSALM 147:7-11

Rain for Everyone

*The Bible says, "He sends rain on the righteous
and the unrighteous."*
MATTHEW 5:45

Who does God give His rain to? Is it only to good people? Or does God's rain come so that everyone can have it and enjoy it?

Yes, God sends His rain to everyone, both good and bad. God is always kind to everyone. He is always doing good things for everyone. He always loves everyone, because God is love.

So you and I should always love everyone too. We should love even the people who are bad to us. Has someone been bad to you? If so, how can you show love to that person?

LISTEN TO JESUS IN MATTHEW 5:43-47

Showers of Blessing

God says, "I will send down showers in season;
there will be showers of blessing."
EZEKIEL 34:26

When the rain comes down in showers, it's like a picture of all the good things God does for us. It is like a picture of all the good gifts God gives to you and me.

He gives us air to breathe, and every heartbeat that keeps us alive. He gives us food to eat and clothes to wear. He gives us people who love us, and the place we call Home. He forgives us when we do what is wrong and bad. He gives us His Son Jesus to save us from our sins. He lets us live forever.

Every time you see the rain, remember your good gifts from God.

READ AND REMEMBER JAMES 1:17

The Good Shepherd

Jesus says, "I am the good shepherd."
JOHN 10:11

Jesus is our Good Shepherd. We are like His sheep. He gives His sheep everything they need. He gives His sheep good green grass to eat. He lets them drink cool water from a quiet stream. He always shows them the right path to take.

With His shepherd's stick, He protects His sheep. We have no need to be afraid, no matter where He takes us.

So be glad, and praise Jesus. Praise and thank Him that He is your Good Shepherd.

READ AND ENJOY PSALM 23

The Good Shepherd

Jesus says, "The good shepherd lays down his life for the sheep."
JOHN 10:11

A good shepherd will always protect his sheep. He will not let any wild beast get them. If a wolf or a lion or a bear comes after the sheep, the good shepherd will fight those wild animals himself. He would rather die than let anyone attack and kill his sheep.

Jesus is our Good Shepherd. He laid down His life for us. He died for us, so that Satan, the wild beast, could not get us.

So be glad, and praise Jesus. Praise and thank Him for saving you from our enemy Satan.

LISTEN TO JESUS IN JOHN 10:1-15

The Good Shepherd

Jesus says, "I am the good shepherd;
I know my sheep and my sheep know me..."
JOHN 10:14

Jesus is our Good Shepherd. He knows everything about us. He calls us by name.

Jesus wants us to hear His voice and know His
love, and love His voice. Then we can follow Him.
He will walk ahead of us on the path, and He will
call us. We will hear Him, and go after Him. He
wants us to stay close to Him.

He keeps us safe. No one can ever take us away
from Him. He will let us live forever. He will take
care of us forever. He will love us forever. And we will have
all of forever to know Him better.

LISTEN TO JESUS IN JOHN 10:27-30

Thirsty for God

In the Bible, David prays, "As the deer pants for streams of water, so my soul pants for you, O God."

PSALM 42:1

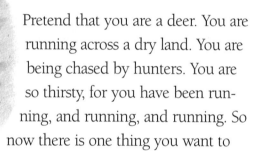

Pretend that you are a deer. You are running across a dry land. You are being chased by hunters. You are so thirsty, for you have been running, and running, and running. So now there is one thing you want to see more than anything else. You want to see a stream of water where you may drink.

This is how we should come to God. We should be thirsty for God. We should be thirsty to hear His words. We should be thirsty to see Him and know Him.

The next time you are thirsty for water, remember to also be thirsty for God.

HEAR DAVID'S PRAYER IN PSALM 42:1-2

Living Water

Jesus says, "Whoever believes in me, as the Scripture has said, streams of living water will flow from within him."
J O H N   7 : 3 8

One day Jesus talked in a loud voice to the people of Jerusalem. He said, "If anyone is thirsty, come to Me and drink!" Jesus also shouted this: "Whoever believes in Me will have rivers of living water flowing from his heart!"

Jesus was talking about the Holy Spirit. When we believe in Jesus, God sends the Holy Spirit to live inside us. The Holy Spirit is like rivers of water that flow from our heart. And this water is alive!

Ask God today to let His living water flow deep and strong from inside you.

LISTEN TO JESUS IN JOHN 7:37-39

Water of Life

In the Bible, John says, "The angel showed me the river of the water of life, as clear as crystal..."
REVELATION 22:1

Someday soon we will see our new home. It is the New Jerusalem, the city coming down out of heaven from God.

In that city there will be a river. It is the river of the water of life. This river will have the clearest water you and I have ever seen. The river will begin at the throne of God and the throne of Jesus. The river will flow down the middle of the widest street in the city. Just seeing it will make everyone glad.

This is the river you will play in when you go to live in that city. But even right now you can tell God "Thank You" for letting you come there to enjoy it someday.

READ AND REMEMBER PSALM 46:4

Strong as an Ox

The Bible says, "From the strength of an ox comes an abundant harvest."
PROVERBS 14:4

In Bible times, God's people used big cows called "oxen" to do lots of hard work. The oxen would pull big wagons. The oxen would pull the plows that farmers used to get their fields ready to grow crops. The oxen were strong.

We have lots of hard work to do, too. So we must be strong. Who can make us as strong as we need to be? God can. In the Bible, God says, "I will strengthen you and help you" (Isaiah 41:10).

For doing the work God wants us to do, God can make us as strong as an ox.

TAKE A LOOK AT 1 CORINTHIANS 1:8

Strong Together

The Bible says this about God's people:
"They have the strength of a wild ox."
NUMBERS 23:22

God makes His people strong. Everyone who believes in Jesus and loves Jesus is a part of God's family, and God's family is strong. All together, we are as strong as wild oxen.

Where I am weak, you are strong. Where you are weak, I am strong. And where both of us are weak, someone else in God's family is strong. God makes us strong all together.

We are strong because God Himself is with us, and He is mighty and powerful. We are weak, but He is strong. So be glad and praise God that He is so mighty.

READ 2 CORINTHIANS 12:10

Take His Yoke

Jesus says, "Take my yoke upon you
and learn from me…"
MATTHEW 11:29

In the old days, oxen would pull a plow or a wagon. Two oxen walked together, side by side. A big piece of wood was fastened across their necks. It was called a yoke. The yoke kept the two oxen together. The plow or the wagon was attached to the yoke. The oxen wore the yoke and walked ahead, pulling the wagon or plow.

Jesus wants to be beside us in the work God has for us to do. So He tells us to wear His yoke. His yoke is easy to wear. And with Jesus beside you to help, our hard work is not too hard.

Ask Jesus to show you how to wear His yoke today.

LISTEN TO JESUS IN MATTHEW 11:28-30

Free from Chains

The Bible says, "I am your servant…you have freed me from my chains."
PSALM 116:16

In the old days, prisoners were sometimes put in chains. The chains went around their arms or feet, to keep them from getting away.

One day a bad king named Herod put the good man Peter in prison. Peter was telling everyone about Jesus, and Herod did not like this. In prison, Peter was put in chains. He was guarded by soldiers. But God's people were praying for Peter.

One night an angel woke up Peter. Peter's chains fell off. The angel led Peter around the soldiers and out of prison. Peter was free! So give praise to God that He does miracles like this.

READ THE STORY IN ACTS 12:1-19

Chains for Christ

In the Bible, Paul says, "I am in chains for Christ."
PHILIPPIANS 1:13

Paul was a man in the Bible who believed in Jesus, and loved Jesus, and told everyone he could about Jesus. But some bad men did not like this. They put Paul in prison, and kept him in chains.

Paul was in prison for a long time. Did that make Paul sad or afraid? No! Paul was brave and strong and glad. Even in prison he still kept telling everyone about Jesus. He would not let those chains bother him. Tell God "Thank You" that you are not in chains.

Now, who can you talk to about Jesus, just as Paul did?

READ CAREFULLY PHILIPPIANS 1:7-19

Chains for the Devil

In the Bible, John says, "I saw an angel...
holding in his hand a great chain."
REVELATION 20:1

We have an enemy, and that enemy is Satan, the devil. Satan hates God. Satan also hates us. He tries to hurt us, because we belong to God, and God loves us.

God is much stronger than Satan. God lives in us, and will protect us from Satan's attacks.

One day a mighty angel from God will come and put chains around the devil. He will throw Satan into prison. Satan will be there for a thousand years. He will come out again for just a short while. But then God will throw the devil into a lake of fire. Satan will stay there forever. So praise God that someday Satan will never bother us again.

READ REVELATION 20:1-10

Jesus Makes a Whip

The Bible says, "Jesus made a whip out of cords..."
JOHN 2:15

Cords are like small ropes. Jesus once made a whip out of cords. He did it in Jerusalem, in the temple. Jesus made the whip. Then He used it to chase away people who were doing wrong and selfish things in God's temple. Jesus called the temple "My Father's house." He told these people that they should not do wrong, selfish things there.

Wherever Jesus comes, He comes to clean out what is wrong and selfish.

Is there anything wrong and selfish that should be cleaned out of your heart, or out of your room, or out of your house? Remember that you and your room and your house belong first to God.

READ THE STORY IN JOHN 2:12-17

A Strong Cord

The Bible says, "A cord of three strands is not quickly broken."
ECCLESIASTES 4:12

Cords and ropes are made of strands twisted together. A rope or cord made of two strands is much stronger than a strand by itself. A rope made of three strands is much stronger still.

The Bible says that it is not good to be alone. It is better to have a good friend. Then you and your friend can help one another. You will be stronger together.

But a rope of three strands is stronger yet. And God is the best Person to be the strand who holds you together. The next time you see a rope, remember how you and your friends and God can be strong together.

READ ECCLESIASTES 4:8-12

Rescued with Ropes

The Bible says, "They pulled Jeremiah up with the ropes and lifted him out of the cistern."
JEREMIAH 38:13

In the Bible, the good man Jeremiah loved God, and spoke God's words. But some people did not like him. They tied him up and dropped him down into a deep, muddy well. Jeremiah had no way to climb out, and no way to get food. His enemies wanted him to die there.

But a good man named Ebed heard what had happened. Ebed got other men to help him. They dropped a rope down to Jeremiah in the well. They carefully pulled him out. Jeremiah did not die in the deep well.

Remember that God always knows how to rescue us, when we are in danger.

READ THE STORY IN JEREMIAH 38:1-13

Noah Builds an Ark

The Bible says, "By faith Noah…in holy fear built an ark to save his family."
HEBREWS 11:7

Noah was a good man. Noah knew how to do what was right, and he did it. In those days, other people who lived in the world were not as good as Noah. They only wanted to do wrong things. But Noah wanted to do right things.

God told Noah to build a big boat — an ark. God told Noah how to do it. Noah obeyed God. He did everything the way God told him to.

What does God want you to do? Are you doing it the way God wants you to?

READ THE STORY IN GENESIS 6:5-22

Into the Ark

God said to Noah, "Go into the ark, you and your whole family…"
GENESIS 7:1

After Noah built the ark, God told him to take his family
inside it. God also brought many animals to Noah — at least
two of every kind of animal on the earth. God told Noah to
bring them on the boat. So Noah did. God also told Noah to
bring enough food on the boat for everyone. Noah did this
too. Noah obeyed God in every way. Noah shows us how
good and right it is to obey God.

When the rain began falling, and
flood waters began rising, surely
Noah was glad that he had obeyed
God!

When you obey God, you will
also be glad. You will never be sorry
for obeying God.

READ THE STORY IN GENESIS 7:1-16

Safe in the Ark

The Bible says, "The waters rose…
and the ark floated on the surface of the water."
GENESIS 7:18

Inside the ark, Noah and his family and all those animals were safe. The stormy waters were all around them. But Noah and his family and the animals did not drown. The water did not touch them.

Jesus is like the ark to us. When we believe Him, when we know He is our Friend, and when we ask for His help, it is like living inside Him. A storm may be all around us. Darkness and trouble may be close by. But Jesus will keep us safe.

Inside Jesus, we are safe. The storm and the darkness and the trouble will not touch us.

READ THE STORY IN GENESIS 7:17-24

Patient Dove

The Bible says, "Noah sent out a dove…"
GENESIS 8:8

After the rain stopped falling, Noah and his family and the animals stayed on the ark for a long time. They still had to wait. It took so long for the flood waters to go away. But Noah was patient and faithful.

Noah opened the ark's window and sent out a dove. The dove was patient. She did not find a home, so she came back to the ark. Seven days later Noah sent the dove out again. This time she brought back to the ark a leaf from a tree. Seven days later Noah sent the dove out again. This time she found a place where she could make her new home.

Can you be as patient as Noah and the dove?

READ THE STORY IN GENESIS 8

To Fly Away

In the Bible, David prayed, "Oh, that I had the wings of a dove!
I would fly away…"
PSALM 55:6

Sometimes when we have many troubles, we wish we could fly away like a dove. But we cannot. We must stay, and see how God will help us get through our troubles.

When David felt like flying away, he prayed to God. He prayed in the evening. He prayed in the morning. And he prayed in the middle of the night. He called out loud to God, and God helped him.

You can call out to God any time of the day or night. God is always glad to hear you.

HEAR DAVID'S WORDS IN PSALM 55:16-17

Spirit Like a Dove

*The Bible says, "The Holy Spirit descended on him
in bodily form like a dove."*
LUKE 3:22

Before Jesus began to preach and to teach, He went to a river
— the Jordan River. A good man named John was there.
John helped Jesus dip down into the water, then come back
up. Jesus was baptized.

After Jesus was baptized and came up out of the water,
God spoke out loud from heaven. He said, "This is My Son,
and I love Him." Then God's Holy Spirit came down on
Jesus. As the Holy Spirit came
down, He looked like a dove.

Now Jesus began to preach
and teach. And now, whenever
you and I tell others about Jesus,
we must first have the Holy
Spirit to help us.

READ THE STORY IN MARK 1:9-11

The Big Dragnet

Jesus says, "The kingdom of heaven is like a net that was let down into the lake…"

MATTHEW 13:47

Sometimes the fishermen in Bible days used a big dragnet to catch their fish. They let down the dragnet into the sea. They dragged it through the water. They pulled the net to shore.

The net would be full of many kinds of fish: good fish and bad fish. The fishermen sorted out the fish. They kept the good fish, and threw the bad fish away.

Jesus said this is how it will be with people someday. Angels will sort out the people. Good people can stay with God. Bad people will be sent away to a terrible place that burns with fire. Tell Jesus "Thank You" that He knows how to make you a good fish to keep forever.

LISTEN TO JESUS IN MATTHEW 13:47-50

The Big Dragnet

Jesus says, "The kingdom of heaven is like a net
that was let down…and caught all kinds of fish."
MATTHEW 13:47

We are like fish swimming in the sea. All around us are many other fish, good fish and bad fish.

Jesus says that one day our time in the sea will be over. God's big dragnet will come down into our water and catch us up. If we are like good fish, we will stay with God forever. If we are like bad fish, we will be thrown away into a terrible burning place. That is what Jesus says.

We can be glad that this day is coming. We do not have to be afraid. We can be glad that God's net will catch us up, so we can be with God forever.

LISTEN TO JESUS IN MATTHEW 25:31-46

The Big Dragnet

Jesus says, "Once again, the kingdom of heaven is like a net..."
MATTHEW 13:47

How can we be like the good fish that fishermen catch and keep? We don't want to be like the bad fish that are thrown away. We don't want to be bad like the people who will someday be thrown into the terrible fire. We want to be good, and to stay with God forever. How can we be good like this?

Only Jesus can make us that good. When we believe in Jesus and love Him, God decides right then to keep us forever. Jesus will be our Friend and Teacher. He shows us how to be good. And God sends His Holy Spirit to live inside us. The Holy Spirit will change us from bad to good.

Say "Thank You" to God for doing all this to make us good.

LISTEN TO JESUS IN JOHN 14:26-27

See the Flowers

Jesus says, "See how the lilies of the field grow."
MATTHEW 6:28

Every time you see flowers, remember that it is God who makes them so pretty. He dresses them up in so many different colors. Why do these flowers wear such fine clothes? Is it because they work hard to make them? No. Is it because they have lots of money to shop and to buy fine clothes? No. God gives these fine clothes to the flowers, all for free.

If God takes such good care of the flowers, then we know He will take good care of us as well.

So be glad, praise and thank God for His wonderful care.

LISTEN TO JESUS IN MATTHEW 6:28-30

Beautiful Flowers

Jesus says, "Consider how the lilies grow."
LUKE 12:27

King Solomon was the richest king the people of Israel ever had. He had fancy clothes. Every morning he could put on whatever royal robe he wanted, and he could wear a crown.

But Jesus says that even King Solomon never looked as fine as the beautiful flowers that grow. God Himself gives the flowers their fine clothing. These flowers will never be workers or soldiers or builders or kings. And these flowers never last for very long. But still God makes them beautiful.

God can also make us beautiful, inside and out. Ask Him to do this. And don't forget to tell Him "Thank You."

LISTEN TO JESUS IN LUKE 12:27-28

Think about Flowers

Jesus says, "Consider how the lilies grow."
LUKE 12:27

Jesus tells us to think about the flowers we see. Don't just look at them. Think about them too. Think about how small and weak they are. They cannot fight. They cannot be strong. They cannot protect themselves. But God makes them beautiful.

Think about how quiet and peaceful they are. They do not worry. They do not cry. They do not complain or argue. But God makes them beautiful.

God will take even better care of you than He does of the flowers. He will be strong for you. He will protect you and make you beautiful. So do not worry or complain or argue.

READ AND ENJOY 1 PETER 5:7

The Narrow Gate

Jesus says, "Enter through the narrow gate."
MATTHEW 7:13

Be glad and praise God that He tells us how we can live with Him forever! Living with God forever is what the Bible calls "eternal life."

There is a road that will take us to eternal life. At the beginning of that road is a gate. The gate is not big. Why is it small and narrow? The gate is small and narrow because it is like Jesus. Jesus is the only way that we can go and live with God forever. The only way to go through His gate is to believe in Jesus and love Him. There is no other way that we can start on the road that goes to eternal life.

So praise Jesus that He is our only way to heaven.

LISTEN TO JESUS IN MATTHEW 7:13-14

The Gate Opens

Jesus says, "I am the gate…"
JOHN 10:9

Jesus tells us that He Himself is the gate. Jesus is our gate to eternal life. Eternal life means living with God forever in His heaven.

Jesus is a gate that opens and closes. If we believe in Him and love Him, He opens up His gate and lets us come in. But some people do not believe in Him and love Him. So the gate does not open for them. They cannot go and live with God forever.

Be glad that you believe in Jesus. Be glad that the gate has opened up to you. Praise Jesus and thank Him that He will take you to live with God forever in His heaven.

LISTEN TO JESUS IN JOHN 10:7-9

The Gate to Good

Jesus says, "I tell you the truth, I am the gate for the sheep."
JOHN 10:7

Jesus is our gate to everything good. Jesus is our gate to everything right, and to everything that we will love and enjoy.

When we want to see and know God and love Him better, Jesus is our gate. If we ask Him, He will teach us how to see and love God better. Jesus is a gate that will open and show us.

When we want to love our family and friends better, Jesus is our gate. If we ask Him, He will teach us how to love others better. Jesus is a gate that will open and show us. What can you ask Jesus to show you?

LISTEN TO JESUS IN JOHN 14:13-14

God Gave

The Bible says, "God so loved the world that he gave his one and only Son…"
JOHN 3:16

When a friend gives you a wrapped present, do you say, "How much should I pay you for this gift?"

No. Your fingers tug away at the bow and the ribbons and the wrapping. You open the box inside. You smile when you see what is there. You say, "Oh, thank you!" And your friend smiles.

God is giving you the best gift there is: He will let you live forever in His heaven with Jesus. You could not earn this gift or buy it. It cost more than anyone could ever pay. Jesus bought it for you. And when you say, "Oh, thank You!" — you will make Him smile.

READ AND REMEMBER ROMANS 6:23

Every Good Gift

The Bible says, "Every good and perfect gift is from above,
coming down from the Father…"
JAMES 1:17

The Bible tells us that every wonderful gift we have is from God. So it is good each day to tell Him "Thank You."

Always, always God gives us what is good. God never changes. He will always give us gifts that are good and perfect.

He gives us good and perfect gifts because He wants us to be good and perfect. The way to begin being good and perfect is to thank God for all that He gives you. Will you thank Him now?

Gifts to Use

*The Bible says, "Each one should use
whatever gift he has received to serve others"*
1 PETER 4:10

What should you do with the good gifts you have received?
Should you hide them? No. Should you throw them away?
No. Should you set them down somewhere and forget about
them? Certainly not.

When you receive a good gift, you should use it.

This is how you should use the good gifts
you receive from God: You should use
them to help other people. This will
please God, and other people will give
thanks to God. What good gifts do you
have that you can use to help others?

READ 1 PETER 4:8-11

Horse of Fire

*The Bible says, "Suddenly a chariot of fire
and horses of fire appeared…"*
2 KINGS 2:11

In the Bible, the man Elijah loved God and obeyed God. He went where God told him to go. He did what God told him to do. He said what God told him to say.

Then came the time for Elijah to leave this world. But Elijah did not die as other people do. God sent a chariot and horses to bring Elijah up to heaven. The chariot and horses were bright, like fire. A stormy wind was blowing. And so, Elijah left this world.

Wasn't this a wonderful thing for God to do for Elijah? God will also do wonderful things for you and me.

READ THE STORY IN 2 KINGS 2:11-12

On the Horses' Bells

*The Bible says, "On that day holy to the lord will be
inscribed on the bells of the horses…"*
ZECHARIAH 14:20

The Bible says that a wonderful new
day is coming. On that day, everything
everywhere will be holy to the Lord.
Even the bells that horses wear will
be holy to the Lord. Even our cook-
ing pots will be holy to the Lord.

But what does that mean — "holy to the Lord"? Those
words mean that everything will belong to God. Everything
will be used for God. Everything will be used for doing good.
Nothing will be used for doing bad.

Tell God "Thank You" that this wonderful day is coming.

READ ZECHARIAH 14:20-21

A Different Horse

In the Bible, John says, "There before me was a white horse,
whose rider is called Faithful and True."
REVELATION 19:11

The Bible shows us what the world will see when Jesus comes back. He will ride a white horse. He will come as a great King and a great Soldier. His eyes will be burning bright. He will wear crowns. Every word He speaks will cut sharply like a sword. He will have these names: Faithful and True, and the Word of God, and King of Kings and Lord of Lords.

The armies of heaven will come behind Him. They will wear white robes and will ride white horses.

Tell Jesus now you are glad He is your King, and you are glad He is coming back.

READ THE STORY IN REVELATION 19:11-16

The Promise Picture

*The Bible says, "I have set my rainbow in the clouds,
and it will be the sign…"*
GENESIS 9:13

Noah and his family and all the animals were on the ark for a long time. Finally the flood waters went away. Finally Noah and his family and the animals could come out of the ark.

Then God made a promise to Noah. God said, "I will never again send a great flood to destroy the earth." Then God put something beautiful in the sky: a rainbow! The rainbow was like a picture of God's promise.

The next time you see a rainbow, remember God's promise. Remember that a great flood will never again come to destroy the world.

READ THE STORY IN GENESIS 9:8-17

God's Glory

The Bible says, "Like the appearance of a rainbow...
so was the radiance around him."
EZEKIEL 1:28

In the Bible, God let the good man Ezekiel look up through a hole into heaven. Ezekiel saw many things in heaven. He saw angels and wheels and a beautiful throne. The greatest thing he saw was the glory of God. "The glory of God" means all the light and brightness of God, and all the colors of God.

Ezekiel saw that God is all bright, like fire. All around God there is brightness like a rainbow.

The next time you see a rainbow, remember that the glory around God is all bright and beautiful and colorful.

READ AND ENJOY EZEKIEL 1:25-28

The Throne's Rainbow

The Bible says, "A rainbow...encircled the throne."
REVELATION 4:3

 In the Bible, God's Holy Spirit carried the good man John through a doorway into heaven. The Holy Spirit showed him many things. John saw angels. He saw the throne where God sits as King.

All around God's throne was a rainbow, bright as a jewel. The rainbow was in a circle, all around the throne.

You and I cannot yet go through heaven's door. But God wants us to know what it is like. He wants us to know how beautiful and bright everything is around His throne. Tell God "Thank You" for letting us know this.

READ AND ENJOY REVELATION 4:1-11

Satan the Serpent

The Bible says, "The serpent was more crafty…"
GENESIS 3:1

When God made this world we live in, everything here was good. God made the first man, Adam. He made Adam's wife, Eve. At first, Adam and Eve were always good. They obeyed God.

But then Satan, God's enemy, came to talk with Eve. He looked like a snake. He lied about God. He told Eve that she should disobey God. Eve listened to that snake. She disobeyed God. Then Adam disobeyed God too. Now Adam and Eve were sinners. They were not always good.

The next time you see a snake, remember how sin came into our world. But remember too how Jesus came to take away our sin.

READ THE STORY IN GENESIS 3:1-15

Snake on a Pole

God said to Moses, "Make a snake
and put it up on a pole…"
NUMBERS 21:8

There was a time when all God's people were walking across the desert. They were hot and tired and hungry and thirsty. They started complaining. Suddenly, snakes came and started biting them. The snakes were poisonous. The people got sick, and some of them died.

God told Moses to make a snake and put it on a pole. Moses did this. Now when people were bitten by the snakes, they looked up at the one Moses made on the pole. And they did not die.

Jesus is like that too. When we look up at Jesus and believe in Him and love Him, then we will live forever.

LISTEN TO JESUS IN JOHN 3:14-16

Satan in Prison

The Bible says, "An angel seized the dragon,
that ancient serpent, who is the devil, or Satan…"
REVELATION 20:2

A serpent is like a snake. "Serpent" is another name in the Bible for Satan. Satan is God's enemy. He always tries to trick God's people, and hurt them. He lies to them. He steals and kills.

But God will not let Satan keep doing this. Someday God will throw Satan in prison. After that, God will throw him into a lake that burns with fire. Satan will hurt forever. He will never stop hurting.

Praise God that He is great and good. God will not let Satan win.

READ REVELATION 20:7-10

Go to That Chariot

The Bible says, "Go to that chariot and stay near it."
ACTS 8:29

In the old days, kings and soldiers and many important people rode in chariots pulled by horses.

One day God told a man named Philip to go down a road in the desert. On that road Philip met a man riding in a chariot. The man was reading from the Bible. He could not understand what he was reading. So Philip told the man everything he could about Jesus. The man in the chariot believed in Jesus, and now he was very glad.

Are you ready to tell other people about Jesus?

READ THE STORY IN ACTS 8:26-39

Chariots Can't Save

*The Bible says, "Some trust in chariots and some in horses,
but we trust in the name of the Lord our God."*

PSALM 20:7

In the old days of Bible times, God's people had many enemies. Many times these enemies had huge armies. Their armies often had many soldiers and many chariots and many horses.

But when God's people trusted God — when they loved God, and obeyed Him, and asked for His help — then these enemies would not hurt God's people.

God is stronger than any army. God is stronger than all the chariots of the enemy. So give praise to God and thank Him, because He keeps His people safe.

READ JOSHUA 11:1-9

God Is Coming

*The Bible says, "See, the Lord is coming with fire,
and his chariots are like a whirlwind."*
ISAIAH 66:15

"Look!" the Bible says. "God is coming!" God is coming some-day to punish all the people who will not believe in Him and love Him. God has a great army of angels in heaven. He will send them to punish the bad people in the world who fight against God.

When that day is here, the chariots of God's army will come down in the sky. They will come like a storm. The storm will be full of fire and wind.

Praise God that He is good and mighty, and that He will always be the Winner over His enemies.

READ TOGETHER ISAIAH 66:15-16

Good Friends

The Bible says, "Jonathan gave his robe to David, along with…even his sword, his bow and his belt."
1 SAMUEL 18:4

In the old days, soldiers did not have guns. They carried swords and spears and bows and arrows. These were the soldiers' weapons. The young man Jonathan was one of the bravest soldiers in the Bible. He fought very well against God's enemies. He had a good sword and a good bow for shooting arrows. Jonathan also had a good friend — David. Jonathan knew David would someday be the king over God's people. So Jonathan gave David his sword, soldier's robe, and belt.

Do you have good friends? What good things have you given to them?

READ THE STORY IN 1 SAMUEL 18:1-4

God's Help

The Bible says, "I do not trust in my bow…"
PSALM 44:6

A good soldier is brave, and fights hard. He uses his weapons well. And he takes good care of his weapons, so they will be at their best, and not break.

But a good soldier also knows that only God decides which side will win a battle. A good soldier knows that he must believe in God and love God. He must ask for God's help in the battle against His enemies.

You can be a good soldier for God if you always remember to ask for God's help in everything.

READ PSALM 44:4-8

No More Wars

The Bible says, "He breaks the bow and shatters the spear..."
PSALM 46:9

In this world where we live, there has always been much fighting. There have always been many wars. Men have carried many weapons.

But someday there will be no more wars. Who will make them stop? God Himself will make them stop. God Himself will break apart all the weapons that soldiers use. People will not fight one another any more.

So be glad and praise our mighty God. Praise and thank Him that He will put an end to all our wars.

LISTEN TO GOD IN PSALM 46:8-10

God's Bride

The Bible says, "As a bridegroom rejoices over his bride,
so will your God rejoice over you."
ISAIAH 62:5

Have you been to a wedding? A wedding is a happy time. A woman is there wearing a beautiful white dress. She is smiling. She is the bride.

A man is there called the groom. He smiles too. Today the bride will become his wife. She will come and live with him and always stay with him. So the groom is very glad.

All God's people together are like His bride. We come to live with Him and always stay with Him and belong to Him. So God is very glad. Tell God that you are glad that you belong to Him.

READ AND ENJOY ISAIAH 65:17-19

Wedding of the Lamb

The Bible says, "The wedding of the Lamb has come,
and his bride has made herself ready."
REVELATION 19:7

Jesus is the Lamb of God. The Bible says that someday Jesus the Lamb of God will be like a groom on his wedding day.

He will have a beautiful bride. She will be ready for Him. She will be ready to live with Him and always stay with Him. She will be ready to belong to Him forever. She will be dressed in beautiful white clothes.

Who will be His bride? Everyone who believes in Jesus and loves Him will be a part of His bride. And the bride's white clothes will be all the good things that His people have done. What good thing does Jesus want you to do now?

READ AND ENJOY REVELATION 19:6-9

Beautiful as a Bride

The Bible says, "I saw the Holy City, the new Jerusalem…
prepared as a bride beautifully dressed for her husband."
REVELATION 21:2

On the day we see the New Jerusalem — the city coming down out of heaven from God — it will be like a happy wedding day.

The New Jerusalem is the city where God's people will live. It will be a beautiful city, as beautiful as a bride. It will all be perfectly ready for God. It will be clean and good. God's people there will all be perfectly good and loving and happy. Jesus Himself will make us that way. He died to take away our ugly sin.

So praise God. Praise and thank Him that He will make you clean and good and loving and glad.

READ CAREFULLY EPHESIANS 5:25-32

Fishing for People

Jesus says, "Come, follow me, and I will make you fishers of men."
MATTHEW 4:19

Jesus had friends who were fishermen. They caught fish. They went out in their boats on the water. They had nets for catching the fish. One day Jesus told them, "Follow Me. Come be with Me. Go where I go. Stay where I stay. And I will help you become a new kind of fisherman. You will not fish for fish. You will fish for people."

His friends left their boats and nets. They would not need boats and nets to catch people. They just needed to be with Jesus and learn from Him.

Do you want to learn how to fish for people? Ask Jesus to teach you.

READ THE STORY IN MATTHEW 4:18-22

Fishing for People

Jesus says, "Come, follow me, and I will make you fishers of men."
MARK 1:17

Jesus had many fishermen friends. Jesus taught them how to be fishermen for people. Jesus can also teach this to you. He can teach you to fish for people. Then you can help other people learn about Jesus. You can help them to believe in Him and love Him. You can help them learn to be truly glad inside.

To do this, here is what you must do first: Follow Jesus. Stay as close to Jesus as you can. Listen carefully to everything He says. Remember what He says, and do it.

If you want this, talk to Jesus about it in a prayer.

LISTEN TO JESUS IN JOHN 10:27

Fishing for People

In the Bible, Peter said, "I'm going out to fish…"
JOHN 21:3

After Jesus was killed on the cross, He rose from the dead. Now His friends did not see Him as much. They did not know what to do. So one night they went fishing. But they did not catch any fish all night.

In the morning, a Man stood on the shore, watching. He called out, "Let your net down on the right side of the boat, and you will catch fish." They did this. They caught 153 fish. The fishermen looked closer at the Man on the shore. It was Jesus! He said to them again, "Follow Me." So they did. And they fished for people.

If you want to follow Him too, tell that to Jesus in a prayer.

READ THE STORY IN JOHN 21:1-14

Pleasant Words

The Bible says, "Pleasant words are a honeycomb..."
PROVERBS 16:24

Everyone loves to hear pleasant words. They are just as good as a sweet taste of honey.

You know how to say pleasant words, don't you? Pleasant words are kind words. Pleasant words are gentle. Pleasant words are when you tell someone, "You did a good job." Pleasant words are when you say, "I like being with you." Pleasant words are when you say, "Thank you for helping me." Pleasant words are when you say, "What can I do to help you?" Pleasant words are when you say, "I love you."

Who can you say pleasant words to now?

READ AND OBEY EPHESIANS 4:29

Sweeter than Honey

The Bible says, "The ordinances of the Lord…
are sweeter than honey, than honey from the comb."

PSALM 19:9-10

God's words are pleasant words.
God's words are sweeter than honey.
God's words are not sour. God's
words are not yucky. God's words
are not bitter or rotten. God's words are
good and sweet to hear.

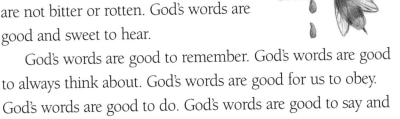

God's words are good to remember. God's words are good
to always think about. God's words are good for us to obey.
God's words are good to do. God's words are good to say and
share with others.

God's words are for us to always enjoy inside us. The next
time you taste some honey, remember how good God's Word is.

READ AND REMEMBER PSALM 119:103

John the Baptist

The Bible says, "John ate locusts and wild honey."
MARK 1:6

In the Bible there was a man named John. We call him John the Baptist. His clothes were made from camel hair. For his food, John ate grasshoppers and wild honey.

John was not a rich man. He did not live in a big fancy house. He did not wear fancy clothes. He did not eat fancy food. He just did what God told him to do.

God had an important job for John. He sent John to get God's people ready for Jesus. How would they get ready? They would get ready by turning away from all the wrong things they were doing. Is there any wrong thing that God wants you to turn away from?

READ JOHN'S STORY IN MATTHEW 3:1-12

Planted by a River

The Bible says, "He is like a tree planted by streams
of water…and whose leaf does not wither."
PSALM 1:3

Trees need water to grow and to keep their leaves green. The land where Jesus lived is a dry land. There is not enough rain to keep green trees growing everywhere.

But there are rivers of water in that land. Trees can grow beside the water. The leaves on those trees are green.

The Bible says that we can be like a tree planted by a river. If you love to hear God's words from the Bible, and if you think about those words in the daytime and at night, then you will be like a tree whose leaves stay green.

READ CAREFULLY PSALM 1

Always Green

The Bible says, "He will be like a tree planted by the water...
its leaves are always green."
JEREMIAH 17:8

How do you know when you are like a tree whose leaves are always green?

You will know you are like this when you keep remembering God. You remember Him even when bad things happen to you. You still remember God. You still believe in Him and love Him. You do not worry. You are not afraid. You know that God will help you. You will be patient and wait for His help. Even when bad things and troubles happen to you, you are glad that you belong to God. You know that He will take care of you. You know that even these bad things are really good things. Are you like this right now?

READ VERY CAREFULLY JEREMIAH 17:7-8

Healing Leaves

*The Bible says, "The leaves of the tree
are for the healing of the nations."*
REVELATION 22:2

Someday we will see the New Jerusalem, the city coming down out of heaven from God.

In that city there will be a river. Beside that river a tree will grow. The tree is the tree of life. The leaves of that tree will be healing leaves. If you were sick, those leaves can make you well. If you were hurt, those leaves can make you better. If you were sad, those leaves can make you happy.

So be glad, and praise God. Praise and thank Him for the tree of life whose leaves can heal.

READ AND ENJOY REVELATION 22:1-2

The Rooster Crows

*Jesus said to Peter, "Before the rooster crows today,
you will deny three times that you know me."*
LUKE 22:34

In the old days in Bible times, people in Jerusalem had roosters. They crowed very early in the morning. One night Jesus was with His friends. He knew that soon He would die. He knew that His good friend Simon Peter would soon tell a lie; that Peter would tell other people that he did not even know Jesus.

Jesus told Peter he would do all this before the rooster crowed in the morning.

It is wrong to lie, and it is wrong to pretend that we do not know Jesus. Jesus knows whenever we do this. Ask Him to help you not to do it.

READ THE STORY IN MATTHEW 26:31-35

The Rooster Crows

The Bible says, "Just as Peter was speaking, the rooster crowed."
LUKE 22:60

Jesus once told Peter that before the rooster crowed in the morning, Peter would lie and pretend he did not know Jesus.

Some soldiers and other men took Jesus away. They were getting ready to kill Jesus. Peter saw the house where the soldiers took Jesus. Peter stood outside. Some people were watching Peter. They said, "You were with Jesus." But Peter said, "No. I do not even know that Man." Peter lied. Suddenly Peter heard a rooster crow. He remembered what Jesus said. He ran away and cried.

Always remember it is wrong to lie, and to say that you do not know Jesus.

READ THE STORY IN MATTHEW 26:69-75

Be Ready

*Jesus says, "You do not know when the owner will come back—
in the evening, or at midnight, or when the rooster crows…"*
MARK 13:35

Long ago, Jesus lived here in our world as a Man. Then He went back to heaven. But He is coming back to our world. When will He come back? We do not know when. It may be early some morning, at the time when the rooster crows. It may be later in the morning, after the sun is up. It may be in the evening, when the sun goes down. It may be late at night, when everything is dark.

All during the day, and all during the night, always remember that Jesus is coming back. And be ready!

LISTEN TO JESUS IN MARK 13:26-37

Shine Like a Star

The Bible says, "Do everything without complaining
or arguing, so that you…shine like stars…"
PHILIPPIANS 2:14-15

Would you like to be as beautiful and sparkly bright as a star in the night sky? The Bible tells us how we can. This is what we must do:

We must do everything without complaining. Yes, we must never complain. And we must do everything without arguing. Yes, we must never argue.

When we complain or argue, it is like being dirty and dark. But when we don't complain or argue, then we are God's children shining like stars. Then we can gladly tell everyone about Jesus. So do not complain or argue.

READ CAREFULLY PHILIPPIANS 2:14-15

Count the Stars

God said to Abraham, "Look up…and count the stars—
if indeed you can count them."
GENESIS 15:5

One night, God spoke to the man in the Bible named Abraham.
Abraham wanted to have some children, but he and his wife
Sarah did not have any.

God took Abraham outside and
said, "Now look up at the heavens.
Count the stars, if you can count them."
There were so many, Abraham could
not count them. And God said, "This
is how many children you will have."

The Bible says that everyone who
believes in Jesus is a child of Abraham.
If you believe in Jesus, you are like a star in the sky that
Abraham saw. You are a star in Abraham's sky.

READ THE STORY IN GENESIS 15:1-6

The Morning Star

Jesus says, "I am…the bright Morning Star."
REVELATION 22:16

Have you ever seen the morning star? It seems to shine brightest in the sky in the time just before the sun comes up in the morning. No other star shines as bright as this one. It is bright and beautiful to see.

Jesus says that He is like the Morning Star. He is bright and beautiful to see. No one else can ever shine as bright as He does.

So be glad, and praise Jesus. Praise and thank Him that He is beautiful and bright like the morning star. And whenever you get up early enough to see the morning star in the sky, make sure you remember to praise Jesus.

READ CAREFULLY 2 PETER 1:19

The Vine

Jesus says, "I am the true vine..."
JOHN 15:1

A vine is the plant where grapes grow. The vine is strong. It grows up from the ground. The vine has many little branches on it. These little branches are where the grapes grow.

But the little branches cannot grow grapes all by themselves. They must be connected to the vine. If you cut off a branch from the vine, the little branch will die. No grapes will grow on that branch.

Jesus says that He is like the vine, and we are like the little branches. If we do not get life from Jesus, we will die. Nothing good can grow from us. Tell Jesus "Thank You" for being our Vine.

LISTEN TO JESUS IN JOHN 15:1-8

The Vine

Jesus says, "I am the vine…"
JOHN 15:5

If a little branch stays connected to the grapevine, it stays healthy. It grows many grapes.

Jesus is the vine. We are the branches. If we stay connected to Jesus, we stay healthy and alive inside. And good things will grow from us. What are these good things?

If we live in Jesus we learn how to love others. We have joy. We have peace. We will be more patient. We will be more kind. We will be good. We will be faithful. We will be gentle. We will have self-control. These are good things that Jesus gives us when we live in Him.

READ AGAIN JOHN 15:1-8

The Vine

Jesus says, "I am the vine…"
JOHN 15:5

Jesus is the vine. You are one of His branches. Jesus wants you to stay with Him and live with Him. Jesus does not want you to cut yourself off from Him. Talk to Him all the time in prayer. Be glad that you know Him and can always pray to Him.

As you pray, listen to Him. Listen for His voice. Remember His words. Remember what He says in the Bible.

Jesus wants you to be alive and healthy inside. You cannot do this by yourself. Only Jesus can keep you alive inside. Only Jesus can keep you healthy inside.

READ AND REMEMBER JOHN 15:1-8

On the Branches

The Bible says, "The birds of the air…
sing among the branches."
PSALM 104:12

Have you seen the branches of the trees when birds are there? Have you heard them sing? Those branches are a wonderful place that God has made. He made tree branches as a good place where birds can sing and squirrels can run and children can climb.

Do you like to climb high in the tree branches? If you do, give thanks to God for making those wonderful places for you and for the birds and for the squirrels.

The next time you're up on a tree branch, remember to thank God.

READ AND ENJOY PSALM 104:10-24

Living in Booths

The Bible says, "The people went out and brought back branches
and built themselves booths..."

NEHEMIAH 8:16

In the old days of Bible times, the people of God had a special holiday. During this holiday time, people went out and cut tree branches. They brought back the branches and put them beside their houses. They built little huts or booths with these branches.

They lived under those branches for seven days. They would eat good food, and they would remember all the good things that God had done for them.

Ask your mother or father if you can cut some tree branches and make a little booth like that. And remember the good things God does for you.

READ THE STORY IN NEHEMIAH 8:14-18

Branch of the Lord

The Bible says, "the Branch of the Lord
will be beautiful and glorious..."
ISAIAH 4:2

The Bible says that Jesus is like a tree branch. He is like the branch of a fruit tree. The branch has green leaves and lots of fruit on it. Jesus is like that.

What fruit do we find on this tree branch? We find the fruit of wisdom, because Jesus is so wise. He knows everything. We find the fruit of understanding, because Jesus understands everything about us. We find the fruit of power, because Jesus is so strong.

The next time you see a tree branch with fruit on it, remember all the good things that Jesus is.

LOOK FOR JESUS IN ISAIAH 11:1-5

Joseph in Prison

The Bible says, "While Joseph was there in the
prison, the Lord was with him…"
GENESIS 39:20-21

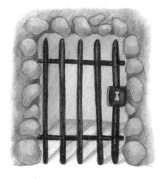

In the Bible, a good man named
Joseph was put into prison one day.
But why was he put there? Isn't prison
a place for people who did something
very wrong? Yes, that is what prisons
are for. It was wrong for the good man
Joseph to be put into prison. But
prison bars cannot keep out God. God was with Joseph. God
helped him. God was kind to and good to Joseph every day
that he was in prison.

And after a long while, Joseph came out of prison.

God is always with us, even when we are wrongly punished
for something we did not do.

READ THE STORY IN GENESIS 39

Singing in Prison

The Bible says, "Paul and Silas were thrown into prison…"
ACTS 16:23

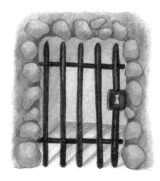

In the Bible, two good men named Paul and Silas were put into prison one day. Paul and Silas had been telling everyone about Jesus. But they were put in prison by men who did not believe in Jesus or love Him.

Paul and Silas did not complain. Night came, and the prison was dark. Paul and Silas were not afraid. They prayed. They sang songs to God. The other prisoners listened to them sing and pray. Suddenly there was an earthquake. The earthquake set all the prisoners free. Paul and Silas got to tell many more people about Jesus.

Who can you tell about Jesus?

READ THE STORY IN ACTS 16:16-34

Free from Prison

The Bible says, "The Lord sets prisoners free…"
PSALM 146:7

God loves us, and He is strong. If we are in prison, He can get us out. He can set us free.

There are many kinds of prisons. Sometimes we do something wrong. Then we do it again and again. We know it is wrong. We want to stop doing it. But it is so hard to stop. We keep on doing what is wrong. It is like being in prison.

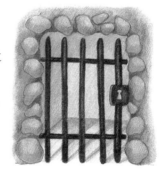

But God can set us free from that prison. God can help us stop doing what is wrong, when we ask Him to help us. Are you asking for His help?

LOOK AT PSALM 142:7

Like an Arrow

The Bible says, "Like arrows in the hands of a warrior
are sons born in one's youth."
PSALM 127:4

Every child is like an arrow. The arrow is kept ready. And one day, the time will come for the arrow to be sent away. The arrow will fly to a new place.

One day when you grow up, you will leave your home and go to a new place.

Every child grows up and does this someday. But be glad that our parents and grandparents and teachers will help us get ready. They help us fly as a straight arrow, and not crooked. They help send us to the new place where God wants us to go.

READ PSALM 127:3-5

Lightning Arrows

The Bible says, "The Lord will appear…
his arrow will flash like lightning."
ZECHARIAH 9:14

Our God is a mighty warrior. His arrows are like lightning.

The Lord is stronger than any enemy. He is stronger than the biggest and loudest storm you have ever seen.

The Lord our God is stronger than a thousand armies and all their weapons. The Lord who loves us is stronger than a million arrows or bombs or rockets.

So be glad, and praise God! Praise and thank Him for His mighty power. Be glad that you are on His side.

READ ZECHARIAH 9:14-16

Arrows on Fire

The Bible says, "Take up the shield of faith, with which you can extinguish all the flaming arrows of the evil one."
EPHESIANS 6:16

Our enemy is the evil one. His other names are Satan and the devil.

He is our enemy because he is God's enemy. The devil hates God, and he hates us. Sometimes the devil tries to make us think about bad things. Sometimes the devil tries to make us worry. He tries to make us not believe in God and not love God.

All these bad thoughts are like arrows that the devil shoots at us. The arrows are on fire. But if we will keep believing in God and loving Him, we will put out the fire on each one. Never stop believing in God!

READ AND REMEMBER EPHESIANS 6:16

All in a Basket

The Bible says, "Who has held all the dust of the earth in a basket?"
ISAIAH 40:12

How much dirt and dust is there in all the world? If you put it all together in one place, how big would the pile be? It would be huge, of course! It would be bigger than any mountain ever was.

But God is so much bigger than that. If He were to pile together all the world's dirt and dust, to Him it would only be like a basketful.

God is so very, very great! Everything that seems big to us is only small to Him. So be glad and give thanks for the greatness of our God.

READ ISAIAH 40:12-15

Baskets for Leftovers

The Bible says, "The disciples picked up twelve basketfuls of pieces that were left over."

LUKE 9:17

Once a huge crowd was listening to Jesus teach. Soon they became hungry. But they had no food.

The twelve disciples of Jesus could find only five loaves of bread and two fish. But Jesus turned it into enough food to feed the whole crowd. He made so much food that there were lots of leftovers. Jesus did not want to waste the leftovers. He sent His friends around with baskets to pick up the leftovers.

Nothing that Jesus gives us should ever be wasted. What has Jesus given you that should not be wasted?

READ THE STORY IN LUKE 9:12-17

Escape in a Basket

*In the Bible, Paul says, "I was lowered in a basket
from a window in the wall..."*
2 CORINTHIANS 11:33

In the Bible, the man Paul was a good teacher. He told people everywhere about Jesus. Paul was always in danger, because many people were enemies of Jesus.

When Paul was younger and his name was Saul, he visited the city of Damascus. The enemies of Jesus there decided to kill Saul. But Saul's friends helped him. First they put him in a big basket. Then they lowered him down the outside of the big wall that went around Damascus. So God helped Paul escape.

God can help you escape from danger too, as you remember to tell others about Jesus.

READ THE STORY IN ACTS 9:19-25

Ten Silver Coins

Jesus says, "Suppose a woman has ten silver coins..."
LUKE 15:8

Coins are money. Coins will buy things. So we like to have coins. And we do not like to lose them.

Jesus tells a story about coins: A woman had ten coins. They were silver, and you could buy a lot with each one. But she lost one of the coins. She had to look all over for it. When she finally found it, she told all her friends and neighbors. They were all glad, and the woman was glad.

Until we believe in Jesus, we are all like a lost coin. But God and His angels are very glad when we believe in Jesus and love Him. Then we are not lost anymore.

LISTEN TO JESUS IN LUKE 15:8-10

Two Small Coins

*The Bible says, "A poor widow came and put
in two very small copper coins…"*
MARK 12:42

One day Jesus went to the temple in Jerusalem. The temple was the place where people came to worship God.

Jesus saw many people there who were giving money to God. Rich people put in lots of money. But they still had a lot of money left. They had lots of money to keep for themselves.

Then Jesus saw a poor woman. She had two small pennies. This was the only money she had. But she gave those pennies to God. She gave God everything she had.

What can you give to God?

Thirty Silver Coins

The Bible says, "They counted out for Judas thirty silver coins."
MATTHEW 26:15

There was a man in the Bible named Judas. He went everywhere with Jesus and His friends. He heard the good things Jesus said. He saw the good things Jesus did. But Judas loved money more than he loved Jesus.

Judas went to some men who wanted to kill Jesus. Judas said to them, "I can tell you how to catch Jesus. How much money will you give me?" These enemies gave Judas thirty silver coins. Then Judas helped them catch Jesus, and they killed Jesus.

So Judas has been sent to the terrible place that is always burning. He cannot live with God, because he did not love Jesus.

READ MATTHEW 26:14-16

God and Lightning

The Bible says, "His lightning lights up the world."
PSALM 97:4

Our God is the God of lightning. He is strong and mighty and powerful like lightning. He is blazingly bright like lightning. And His voice is strong and loud, stronger and louder than lightning.

Have you seen the lightning flash? Have you heard the sound of its thunder? Every time you see the lightning and hear its thunder, remember God. Remember how strong and mighty and bright He is. Remember that God has sent us His lightning to help us know what He is like.

God is gentle and loving. But He is also mighty and bright, like lightning. Praise God today for all that He is.

READ AND UNDERSTAND PSALM 97:1-6

Jesus and Lightning

*Jesus says, "The Son of Man in his day will be like the lightning,
which flashes and lights up the sky from one end to the other."*
LUKE 17:24

Jesus says that when He comes back to the world, He will seem like lightning.

Yes, He will come like lightning! Lightning does not come slowly. Lightning comes suddenly. Lightning comes fast! Jesus will come suddenly, too. Jesus is fast!

When lightning comes, it lights up all the sky and all the ground. Everyone all around can see it. When Jesus comes, everyone all around will see Him. He will light up the sky and all the ground. So be glad, and praise Jesus that He will come like lightning.

LISTEN TO JESUS IN MATTHEW 24:27

Lightning in Heaven

The Bible says, "From the throne came flashes of lightning,
rumblings and peals of thunder."
REVELATION 4:5

God let the good man John take a look into heaven. God's Spirit carried John through a doorway in the sky. John saw God's throne where God sits as the King.

Lightning was flashing from the throne. John saw this. And John heard the thunder rumble and crack.

Yes, God is awesome and powerful! God is mighty! Only God can make the lightning and thunder that come from the clouds. And we will see God's lightning and thunder in heaven. So be glad, and praise God for His mighty power.

TAKE A LOOK AT REVELATION 11:19

Tablets of Stone

God said to Moses, "I will give you the tablets of stone, with the law and commands I have written..."
EXODUS 24:12

In the Bible, God asked the good man Moses to come up on a high mountain and meet with Him. So Moses went up on the mountain. There was lightning and thunder on the mountain, and fire and smoke. The mountain shook with an earthquake.

God talked with Moses on the mountain. God told Moses the right rules for His people to obey. God Himself wrote down some of these rules on two heavy, flat pieces of stone. These stones were called tablets.

God always knows the right rules for His people to obey. Today these rules are written down in the Bible, so we can learn and understand them.

READ TOGETHER EXODUS 32:15-16

Ten Commandments

The Bible says, "The Lord gave Moses the two tablets of stone inscribed by the finger of God."
EXODUS 31:18

When Moses was up on God's mountain, God gave him two tablets of stone. The tablets had words written on them. These words were the right rules for God's people. There were ten rules written down on the tablets. We call these rules the Ten Commandments.

The Ten Commandments told God's people that they must especially do two things: First, they must love and worship God. Second, they must love one another, and never hurt one another.

This is what God wants all His people to do. Will you remember these two things?

LISTEN TO JESUS IN MATTHEW 22:37-40

Broken Tablets

The Bible says, "His anger burned and he threw the tablets…"
EXODUS 32:19

High on God's mountain, God gave Moses two stone tablets. God's Ten Commandments were written on them. These commandments told God's people to love Him and to love one another.

Moses came down the mountain. He carried the two tablets to God's people. But when he found God's people, they were being bad. They were not loving God and they were hurting one another. Moses was angry. He threw those tablets down to the ground. They broke. And God was even more angry than Moses.

Remember that to please God, we must love Him and love one another. Jesus helps us do this, so that God is not angry.

READ EXODUS 34:1-4

A Prayer in a Cave

The Bible says, "When David had fled from Saul into the cave."
PSALM 57

One day the good man David was in a cave. He was hiding from men who were trying to catch him and hurt him. There in the darkness, David prayed. He asked for God's help and protection.

He said he knew God loved him. He said God's love was higher than the sky. He told God he would not be afraid.

David sang to God. He promises that wherever he went, he would praise God.

Can you tell God these things? You can pray David's good prayer, without even hiding in a cave!

READ DAVID'S PRAYER IN PSALM 57

A Prayer in a Cave

The Bible says, "When David was in the cave. A prayer."
PSALM 142

There is another prayer in the Bible that David prayed in a cave. David was hiding again from men who were chasing him. David was tired. He felt weak, not strong. The cave seemed like a prison. So David cried aloud to God. David told God how afraid and troubled and worried he was. He said he felt as if he did not have any friends.

But David knew that God was his friend. David asked God to rescue him and set him free. David promised to tell other people how good God is.

When you feel weak or afraid or worried, you can pray the words that David did.

READ DAVID'S PRAYER IN PSALM 142

Out of the Cave

The Bible says, "Jesus came to the tomb. It was a cave with a stone laid across the entrance."
JOHN 11:38

Jesus had a good friend named Lazarus. Jesus loved Lazarus. But one day while Jesus was away, Lazarus died. Jesus came back to the town where Lazarus had lived with his sisters. The sisters and friends of Lazarus were crying. Jesus cried too.

He went to the place where Lazarus was buried. It was a cave. A huge stone was over the front. Jesus asked some men to take the stone away. Then Jesus shouted, "Lazarus, come out!"

Lazarus obeyed. He was not dead any more. Jesus made him alive. Always remember that Jesus is stronger than death. He makes his friends come back to life.

READ THE STORY IN JOHN 11:17-44

God's Ice

The Bible says, "The breath of God produces ice…"
JOB 37:10

The weather outside may be warm today. But can you remember a time in the winter when the wind was cold, and ice was everywhere outside? It is God who makes the weather cold or hot. The ice and the cold wind that God sends are ways to show us His power. Even on a warm day, God could send an icy wind if He wanted to.

The next time you have ice in a drink, remember the winter ice that God makes. Remember how He sends His cold wind. Praise and thank Him for this, and for warm summer days as well!

READ AND THINK ABOUT JOB 37:9-10

The World's Weather

The Bible says, "Who can withstand his icy blast?"
PSALM 147:17

On this summer day, remember again the icy storm that comes from God in the winter.

We can praise the Lord for all the different kinds of weather He sends. He shows us His power in so many different ways. He tells the world's weather what to do. The world's weather obeys Him. The weather shows us how awesome God is, and how He can make so many different things.

So be glad, and praise God. Praise and thank Him for His wonderful power we see every day in the weather.

READ AND ENJOY PSALM 147:15-18

Icy Sky

The Bible says, "Above the heads of the living creatures was what looked like an expanse, sparkling like ice, and awesome."
EZEKIEL 1:22

God once made an opening in heaven so the good man Ezekiel could look through. Ezekiel saw angels and wheels, and God's throne, and God's glory.

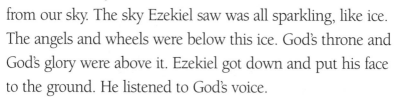

Ezekiel also saw what looked like a sky. It was different from our sky. The sky Ezekiel saw was all sparkling, like ice. The angels and wheels were below this ice. God's throne and God's glory were above it. Ezekiel got down and put his face to the ground. He listened to God's voice.

When we want to think about how awesome God is, we can also kneel and worship Him, and listen for His voice.

TAKE A LOOK AT EZEKIEL 1:22-28

Mountain Man

The Bible says, "When Jesus saw the crowds,
he went up on a mountainside..."
MATTHEW 5:1

One day Jesus was in the land called Galilee. Galilee has many hills and mountains. Jesus walked up one of the mountains. He sat down. His friends followed Him and came close. Soon many more people came too. They listened, because Jesus was teaching His friends many things.

He told them how they could be truly happy. He was saying, You might be poor now, but someday your home will be heaven. You may be sad now, but someday God will comfort you. You may feel weak, but someday you will be strong enough to own the world.

Only God can truly make you happy. And He will do it.

LISTEN TO JESUS IN MATTHEW 5:1-5

Mountain Man

The Bible says, "Jesus went up on a mountainside and sat down. His disciples came to him..."
MATTHEW 5:1

On a mountain in Galilee, Jesus taught His friends. He said, You may be hungry and thirsty now to know and do what is right. So God will fill you full. You may be busy now helping others. So God will help you.

If you are clean inside, you will see God. If you help others not to argue and fight, people will say you are God's child. If other people hurt you because you believe in Jesus and love Him, you can still be glad. You will be given a wonderful prize in heaven.

So praise and thank Jesus that He will make you truly happy.

LISTEN TO JESUS IN MATTHEW 5:6-12

Mountain Man

The Bible says, "The disciples went to Galilee,
to the mountain where Jesus had told them to go."
MATTHEW 5:1

One day Jesus' friends went up again on a mountain in Galilee. Jesus was waiting for them. Soon Jesus was going back to Heaven. Before He left, He wanted to talk with His friends.

He was saying, I am in charge of everything in the world and in heaven. Go and teach people everywhere how to believe in Me and love Me. Show them how God and Jesus and the Holy Spirit can make them clean inside. Teach them to obey everything I say to do. And I will be with you — all day long, every day, forever.

How can you obey what Jesus said that day?

LISTEN TO JESUS IN MATTHEW 28:16-20

Living in Tents

The Bible says, "Abraham lived in tents, as did Isaac and Jacob…"
HEBREWS 11:9

In the Bible, the good man Abraham did not build houses or live in a city. Abraham lived in tents. When it was time to move, he took down his tent and carried it. It was easy for Abraham to go wherever God wanted him to go.

Abraham knew that someday he would not live in tents. Someday he would live in a big strong city that will last forever. This city is in heaven.

Wherever you live now is not where you will live forever. God has a better, bigger, stronger home for you. Can you give Him thanks right now for your home in heaven?

READ AND THINK ABOUT HEBREWS 11:8-10

The Tabernacle

The Lord said, "Set up the tabernacle, the Tent of Meeting…"
EXODUS 40:2

There was a time when God's people were all walking across the desert. They were there in the desert for forty years. While they were there, God told them to make a beautiful tent and set it up. The tent was not for people to live in. It was a place where God would come and be with His people. It was where God's people could worship Him.

God told them exactly how to make it and how to set it up. This beautiful tent was called the Tabernacle.

Praise God and thank Him today that God loves His people, and always wants to be with them.

READ THE STORY IN EXODUS 40:17-38

Sky Like a Tent

The Bible says, "He stretches out the heavens like a tent..."
PSALM 104:2

The Bible says that the sky is like a tent. God has stretched it out so high above us.

Isn't it a beautiful tent? Sometimes it is blue. We see a golden ball of fire go slowly across it. Sometimes the tent is gray with clouds. The clouds move and roll, and drop rain and snow. Sometimes the tent is black. We see a silver ball of light go slowly across it. We see little sparkles of light scattered across the black.

And sometimes the tent is only dark. But we know that God made it, and that He is there above it.

TAKE A LOOK AT ISAIAH 40:22

Why Thorns Grow

God says, "The ground will produce thorns and thistles for you…"
GENESIS 3:18

Have you ever had your legs or hands pricked by a thorn? Many thorns grow from the ground. They are there because God sent them as a punishment.

God sent this punishment after Adam and Eve first disobeyed Him. Adam and Eve were the first man and woman on the earth. God made them good. But they chose to be bad. And now, everyone who lives is bad sometimes. Everyone has sinned. Everyone is a sinner.

The next time you see a thorn, remember that everyone is a sinner. But remember also that Jesus came to take away our sins and our punishment. He will also take away the thorns.

READ AND ENJOY ISAIAH 55:12-13

Thorns That Choke

*Jesus says, "Other seed fell among thorns, which
grew up and choked the plants."*
MATTHEW 13:7

Jesus once talked about thorns
when He told a story. In this
story, a farmer had some seed. He
threw the seed everywhere. He
wanted the seed to grow up into some-
thing he and his family could eat. Some of the seed fell where
thorns were. The thorns would not give the seeds any room
to grow.

Jesus said the seeds are like God's words which can grow
up inside us. The thorns are also like something inside us.
The thorns are like our worries and our selfishness. These
things will not give God's words any room to grow.

Are there any thorns inside you that you should pull out?

LISTEN TO JESUS IN MATTHEW 13:22

Crown of Thorns

*The Bible says, "The soldiers twisted together a crown
of thorns and put it on his head."*
J O H N   1 9 : 2

Before Jesus was killed on the cross,
some soldiers beat Him and
laughed at Him. They had heard
that Jesus was called a king. But
He did not look like a king to
them. So they made fun of Him. They took sharp, ugly
thorns, and twisted these thorns together. Then they
smashed the thorns down on Jesus' head. They laughed at
Him, and called these thorns His "crown."

Jesus could have stopped them from doing this. But He
did not. He let the soldiers hurt Him and laugh at Him. And
He let them kill Him, so He could die for their sins.

Remember today to tell Jesus "Thank You."

READ THE STORY IN MATTHEW 27:27-31

God's Path

In the Bible, David prayed, "Show me your ways,
O Lord, teach me your paths."
PSALM 25:4

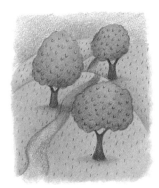

Every day we can ask God, "Show me Your ways, O Lord. Teach me Your paths. Show me the work I can do today for You. Show me the people I can help today."

Do you truly want God to show you where to go and what to do and how to do it? Tell God this, and ask Him.

God will teach you from the Bible. He will lead you through your parents. He will bring you the work He wants you to do, and the people He wants you to help. God does this because He is so good, and because He loves you.

ENJOY READING PSALM 25:4-10

Straight Path

*The Bible says, "In all your ways acknowledge him,
and he will make your paths straight."*
PROVERBS 3:6

The Bible says that when we do wrong things, it is like walking on a crooked path. But God can keep our path straight. A straight path means we are doing what is right and good. We make God happy by what we do and say and think.

On a straight path, you can run fast and free. God can keep it straight and smooth. He will do this if we remember Him all day and in the night.

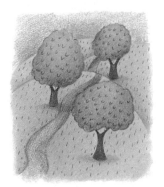

Remember to praise and thank Him for His gifts to you. And ask for His help. God is glad to keep your path straight.

READ AND REMEMBER PROVERBS 3:5-6

No Other Way

Jesus says, "I am the way…"
JOHN 14:6

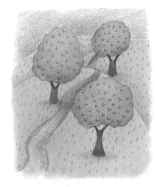

Jesus is the way. Jesus is our straight, smooth path that we can run on. Our Lord Jesus loves us and died for us. He is our way to live forever with God in heaven. Jesus is the only way. There is no other way to heaven, except by believing Jesus and loving Him and walking with Him on the path.

Jesus is the way to everything that is good and right. So be glad, and praise Jesus. Stay close to Him. Tell Him that He is the path you want to run on forever.

LISTEN TO JESUS IN JOHN 14:5-6

Go to the Ant

*The Bible says, "Go to the ant...;
consider its ways and be wise!"*
P R O V E R B S   6 : 6

Ants work hard. Have you seen how they hurry along in their work?

The Bible says that ants are a little picture for us of how hard we should work. We should not be lazy. If you are lazy, you are what the Bible calls a "sluggard." No one wants to be called an awful name like that! So don't be lazy.

The next time you see an ant, remember how hard God wants you to work. When God gives you work to do, do it with all your strength. Ask for God's help. And even when you rest, use your resting time to talk with Him.

TAKE A LOOK AT PSALM 105:4

Saving for Later

The Bible says, "The ant stores its provisions in summer and gathers its food at harvest."
PROVERBS 6:8

The ants work hard. They work hard to store up food. They do not eat everything right now. They store some food and save it, so they will have food later. They are wise.

When you get something good, do you know how to save some for later? Or do you hurry and use it all up now? It is better and wiser to save some for later.

If you will do this now with little things, later you will find it easy to do it with big things too. You will be glad that you learned this good lesson.

READ PROVERBS 6:6-11

Stored Up Treasures

The Bible says, "Ants are creatures of little strength,
yet they store up their food in the summer…"
PROVERBS 30:25

The ants work hard to store up good food for later.

Jesus tells us that we also should store up good things for later. He says that we can store up treasures. Right now we can store up treasures for heaven, where we can enjoy them forever. Nothing ever breaks or wears out or gets torn or used up in heaven. Every good thing in heaven lasts forever.

How do we store up these treasures? Jesus Himself will show you. He will bring you people to love and to help and to forgive. He will bring you work to do. Then He will reward you with treasures in heaven.

LISTEN TO JESUS IN MATTHEW 6:19-21

Teaching from a Boat

The Bible says, "He sat down and taught the people from the boat."
LUKE 5:3

Jesus loves to teach. One day He was by the Sea of Galilee. People crowded around Him. They wanted to hear everything He said. Jesus saw some fishing boats. Jesus stepped into Peter's boat. Peter moved it a little further out in the water. Jesus sat down in the boat. Now the people on the shore could see Him and hear Him.

Jesus always finds ways to teach us, so we can see Him better and hear Him better.

The next time you see a boat, remember how much Jesus loves to teach us. Look for Him and listen to Him, and He will teach you many things.

READ THE STORY IN LUKE 5:1-11

A Storm Goes Away

The Bible says, "They got into a boat and set out."
LUKE 8:22

One day Jesus told His friends they were going over to the other side of the Sea of Galilee. They got in a boat and started across the water. Jesus was tired. He went to sleep in the boat.

Suddenly a storm came with a terrible wind. The boat was thrown this way and that. It began filling up with water. But Jesus was still asleep. His friends woke Him up. They were so frightened! They thought they would drown. Jesus stood up and told the wind and water to be still. At once, the storm went away.

So give praise to Jesus that He is stronger than any storm.

READ THE STORY IN LUKE 8:22-25

Walking on Water

The Bible says, "They saw Jesus approaching the boat, walking on the water."
JOHN 6:19

One night Jesus' friends were in a boat on the Sea of Galilee. They could not go fast. The wind blew hard against them.

Late that night, Jesus came out to them. He was walking on the water. He told them who He was. "Don't be afraid," He said.

Peter got permission from Jesus to walk on the water too. Then Peter became afraid and started sinking. But Jesus rescued Him. When Jesus and Peter were back in the boat, the wind stopped. His friends praised Him. They said, "You are the Son of God." We, too, can praise Jesus that He is the Son of God.

READ THE STORY IN MATTHEW 14:22-33

Huge Grapes

The Bible says, "They cut off a branch bearing a single cluster of grapes."
NUMBERS 13:23

God promised to give His people a wonderful new land. God's people could live there and build houses and grow food.

God sent the good man Moses to lead His people to this new land. Before they got there, Moses sent some soldiers ahead to find out what this new land was like. The soldiers found many good things to eat. They brought back some huge grapes. They wanted to show Moses that the land God was giving them was very good. There were many good grapes to eat there, and many other good things.

The gifts God gives us are always good.

READ THE STORY IN NUMBERS 13:17-25

Kind to the Poor

The Bible says, "Do not pick up the grapes that have fallen.
Leave them for the poor…"
LEVITICUS 19:10

God's people could grow many good things in the Promised
Land God gave them. They could grow lots of good grapes
— sweet and juicy.

God wanted them to grow as much good fruit as they
wanted. He wanted them to enjoy these good things. He also
wanted them to remember people who
were poor. So He told His people not to
take all the grapes for themselves. He
told them to leave some there so poor
people could come and get them.

God is kind to the poor. He wants His
people to be kind to the poor. What can
you do to be kind to the poor?

READ DEUTERONOMY 24:19-21

Still Loving God

The Bible says, "Though there are no grapes on the vines…
yet I will rejoice in the Lord…"
HABAKKUK 3:17-18

God's people lived in the Promised Land. But they did not always obey God there. They did what was wrong and bad. God loved them and helped them and told them to be good. But they kept doing what was wrong. God had to punish them. He sent enemies who hurt them and hurt their land.

Habakkuk was a good man who talked with God about this. Habakkuk decided he would still believe in God and love God, even if there were no more grapes in the Promised Land, or any other food.

Would you believe in God and love Him, even if you had nothing to eat?

READ HABAKKUK 3:17-18

After the Lion

In the Bible, David says, "I have killed both the lion and the bear…"
1 SAMUEL 17:36

The boy David was a shepherd. He took care of sheep. He protected them from lions and bears. God made David strong and brave.

When a lion came and carried off a sheep in its mouth, David ran after it. He hit the lion and rescued the sheep from the lion's mouth. When the lion turned and attacked David, David fought back and killed it.

David knew that God made him strong and brave. When we are truly strong and brave, it is God who makes us that way. So be glad and give thanks to God that He can do this for you.

READ ABOUT DAVID IN 1 SAMUEL 17:34-37

Like a Roaring Lion

The Bible says, "Your enemy the devil prowls around like a roaring lion…"
1 P E T E R   5 : 8

The Bible says that our enemy the devil is like a lion. The lion roars and goes looking for someone to capture.

We are like sheep that the devil wants to catch and eat. But Jesus is like the shepherd boy David. Jesus goes to the lion and rescues His sheep from the lion's mouth. Then He kills the lion.

Our enemy the devil roars and attacks. But our Jesus is stronger than the devil. Jesus helps us, so that the devil will not hurt us. And someday the devil will be destroyed. Praise Jesus today that He is stronger than the devil.

READ CAREFULLY 1 PETER 5:8-9

Jesus the Lion

The Bible says, "See, the Lion of the tribe of Judah,
the Root of David, has triumphed."
REVELATION 5:5

The Bible tells us many names for Jesus. We call Him Lord and Savior and King and Teacher and Shepherd. The Bible calls Jesus the Bread of Life, and the Light of the World, and the Gate, and the Morning Star, and the Vine, and the Way. The Bible says our Jesus is the Lamb of God.

The Bible also calls Him the Lion. He is the Lion of the Tribe of Judah. He is mighty and strong like a lion. He is awesome. He is never, ever afraid.

Jesus loves it when you know His many names, and call Him by those names. Remember to do this.

READ REVELATION 5:1-10

Climbing a Tree

*The Bible says, "Zacchaeus ran ahead
and climbed a sycamore-fig tree to see Jesus."*
LUKE 19:4

Give thanks to God for trees! A tree is good for many things. It is where birds and squirrels can build a home. It gives us shade from the hot sun. And it is something high where we can climb and see better.

In the Bible, the man Zacchaeus once climbed a tree. He wanted to see Jesus better. And sure enough, he did.

The next time you climb a tree, think about Jesus up there. Talk with Him and praise Him. In your heart, He will let you see Him better.

READ THE STORY IN LUKE 19:1-10

Under a Tree

Jesus said to Nathanael, "I saw you under the fig tree."
JOHN 1:50

In the Bible, a man named Nathanael was under a shade tree. This was a good place to be on a hot, sunny day. Another man named Philip came and found Nathanael. Philip told Nathanael about Jesus. "Come and see Him," Philip said.

Nathanael went to see Jesus. Nathanael did not know Jesus. But Jesus already knew about Nathanael. Jesus said to him, "I saw you while you were under the tree."

The next time you are under a shade tree, remember that Jesus knows all about you. And He loves you.

READ THE STORY IN JOHN 1:43-51

Under a Tree

The Bible says, "Every man will sit...under his own fig tree,
and no one will make them afraid."
MICAH 4:4

The Bible tells us about a wonderful time that is coming for God's people. Everyone will be able to sit and rest under shade trees, and they will never again be afraid.

People from all over the world will come to God, so God can teach them. They will all listen carefully to what God says. People will not fight one another anymore. God will help them all be friends.

So be glad, and praise God. Praise and thank Him for these wonderful days that are coming for the people of God.

READ AND ENJOY MICAH 4:1-5

Under His Wings

Jesus said, "How often I have longed to gather your children together, as a hen gathers her chicks under her wings..."

MATTHEW 23:37

People in Jerusalem wanted Jesus killed on the cross. But Jesus loved these people. When He came to this city where He would be killed, He told them how much He loved them. He said how much He wanted to gather these people together, just as a mother hen gathers her chicks under her wings. Jesus wanted to care for all these people and protect them. They would not listen to Him and asked that He be killed.

Jesus still showed His love for them. He died on the cross for their sins. Tell Jesus "Thank You" that His love for us never ends.

LISTEN TO JESUS IN LUKE 13:34-35

Six Wings

The Bible says, "Above him were seraphs, each with six wings"
ISAIAH 6:2

In the Bible, God let the good man Isaiah see into heaven. Isaiah saw the Lord seated on His throne. He also saw angels called seraphs. Each one had six wings. With two wings they covered their faces. (This helps us remember how bright God's glory is.) With two other wings the seraphs covered their feet. (This helps us see how humble and polite they were before God.) With two other wings, the seraphs flew.

The angels kept calling out to one another, "Holy, holy, holy is the Lord Almighty." These seraphs worshiped God with their wings and with their voices.

What can you and I worship God with?

READ ISAIAH 6:1-4

Six Wings

The Bible says, "Each of the four living creatures had six wings…"
REVELATION 4:8

One day God's Spirit carried the good man John through a doorway into heaven. John got to see God's throne with a rainbow and lightning and thunder all around it.

John also got to see four living creatures, which were like angels. Each one had six wings. One creature was like a lion, one was like an ox, one had a face like a man, and one was like a flying eagle. The creatures kept saying, "Holy, holy, holy is the Lord God Almighty." They always praise God.

How can you and I keep praising God?

Into the Tomb

*The Bible says, "Where Jesus was crucified,
there was a garden, and in the garden a new tomb…"*
JOHN 19:41

After Jesus was killed on the cross, His friends were afraid they would not see Him alive again.

A good man named Joseph took down the dead body of Jesus from the cross. A man named Nicodemus helped him. Joseph and Nicodemus wrapped Jesus' body in a cloth like a sheet. They carried away Jesus' body and laid it in a tomb. It was carved from rock, like a cave. Joseph and Nicodemus rolled down a big stone over the front of the tomb. No one could get in or out without pushing up that heavy stone.

Always remember that Jesus really did die, and was buried.

READ LUKE 23:50-54, JOHN 19:38-42

Watching the Tomb

*The Bible says, "The women...saw the tomb
and how his body was laid in it."*
LUKE 23:55

Jesus died. Then Jesus was buried in a tomb. Some women
that day were watching while Joseph and Nicodemus put
Jesus' body in the tomb. The women saw where He was
buried. They wanted to come back later to cover the dead
body of Jesus with perfume and spices. This was how they
could show their love for Jesus.

They did not come back on the morning after Jesus was
buried. This day was when people rested. So the women
waited until the next morning to
come back.

What can you and I do to
show our love for Jesus?

READ LUKE 23:55-56

Empty Tomb

The Bible says, "The women took the spices…
and went to the tomb."
LUKE 24:1

Jesus had died, and was buried. Some women who loved Jesus had seen how He was buried.

Early on a Sunday morning, the women walked to the tomb. They had spices and perfume to put on Jesus' body, to show their love for Him. They wondered how they could get inside the tomb, because a big stone was over the front.

But when they got there, the stone was already rolled away. An angel told them the wonderful truth. Jesus was risen from the dead! He was not dead anymore. He is alive forever. He is alive, and you and I can talk to Him this very moment.

READ LUKE 24:1-8

Water for Camels

In the Bible, Rebekah said,
"I'll draw water for your camels too…"
G E N E S I S   2 4 : 1 9

Rebekah was a kind young woman in the Bible.

One evening she went to the well where the people from her town got water. She filled a jar with water and began carrying it home. But a stranger was there, tired and thirsty. He had camels with him. He asked Rebekah for a drink of water from her jar. Rebekah gave him a drink. Then she said, "I'll give water to your camels too." With her jar, she brought water for all the camels. She was kind to the man and kind to his animals.

What is something kind you can do for someone soon?

READ THE STORY IN GENESIS 24:10-27

Camels Approaching

The Bible says, "As Isaac looked up,
he saw camels approaching."
GENESIS 24:63

Isaac was the son of the good man Abraham. But Isaac's mother had died. Isaac was sad.

One day Isaac was alone, out in a field. He looked up. Many camels were coming. Isaac went closer to meet them. Riding one of the camels was a beautiful young woman. She was Rebekah. She had come to be Isaac's wife. God had chosen her to be Isaac's bride. So Isaac and Rebekah were married. And now, Isaac was not so sad anymore.

When we are sad, God will be kind to us. So never stop believing in Him and loving Him.

READ THE STORY IN GENESIS 24:62-67

Rich People

*Jesus says, "It is easier for a camel to go through a needle's eye
than for a rich man to enter the kingdom of God."*
MARK 10:25

In Bible times, many rich people owned
lots of camels, and other things too.
Some people thought that God
likes rich people more than poor
people. They thought that God
gives more things to rich people
because they are better than poor
people. But Jesus knew this is not true. Jesus said that it is
hard for rich people to believe in God and love Him. Only
God can make this happen. His Holy Spirit can make a rich
person clean inside. Then that person can love God more
than he loves his riches. What things do you own? Do you
love God more than you love these things?

LISTEN TO JESUS IN MATTHEW 19:23-30

He Is Our Shield

The Bible says, "We wait in hope for the Lord;
he is our help and our shield."

PSALM 33:20

God's people in the Bible praised God with a new song that we call Psalm 33. In this song, they praised God that He is their shield.

A shield is a big piece of metal that a soldier carried to protect himself in battle. God is the shield for His people. He protects us and helps us. God saves us from our enemy the devil. If God does all this for us, isn't it right that we should believe in Him, and love Him, and always ask for His help?

Ask God to be your shield, and believe that He will.

READ PSALM 33

He Is My Shield

*In the Bible, David says, "He is my loving God…
my shield, in whom I take refuge…"*
PSALM 144:2

The good man David sang a new song in the Bible that we call Psalm 144. David's enemies were trying to catch him. But in this song, David prayed that God would protect him and rescue him. David asked God to reach down and help him. He said God was his fort, and God was his shield. And David called the Lord, "My loving God."

David promised to sing his new song to God, and to make music to God.

Is God your shield and your helper? What new song can you sing for Him?

HEAR DAVID'S SONG IN PSALM 144

The Shield of Faith

The Bible says, "Take up the shield of faith…"
EPHESIANS 6:16

You and I are in a battle. Our enemy the devil is fighting against God's people. To be God's good soldiers in this battle, we must fight the way the Lord tells us to fight. He is our General and our Captain.

We must also wear the armor God gives us to wear. If we truly believe God is always great and always good to us, we can carry God's special shield. It is the shield of faith. When the devil shoots burning darts at us, our shield will stop them.

So be glad, and tell God "Thank You" for this weapon.

READ AND REMEMBER EPHESIANS 6:16

He Is the Rock

The Bible says, "Oh, praise the greatness of our God! He is the Rock..."
DEUTERONOMY 32:3-4

What is the biggest rock you have ever seen? However big it is, I know one that is bigger.

In the Bible, one of God's names is the Rock. He is bigger and heavier than the biggest, heaviest rock we have ever seen. God protects us, like a fort made of rock or a wall made of rock. God is a strong, heavy rock that we can stand on, and not fall. He is a rock so strong that we can build our house on it.

The next time you see a rock, think about God. Be glad, and praise Him that He is our mighty Rock.

READ AND ENJOY DEUTERONOMY 31:30-32:4

Built on the Rock

Jesus says, "A wise man…built his house on the rock."
MATTHEW 7:24

God is our mighty rock. He is strong enough to build our house on. How do we build our house on this mighty rock? Jesus tells us how. He says we must do two things: First, we must listen to what Jesus says. Second, we must do what Jesus tells us to do.

But what if we only listen to what He says, and forget to do it? If we don't do what Jesus says, it is like building our house on sand. When rain and stormy winds come, our house will fall down.

What does Jesus want you to do now?

LISTEN TO JESUS IN MATTHEW 7:24-29

Water from the Rock

God said to Moses, "Strike the rock, and water
will come out of it for the people to drink."
EXODUS 17:6

God's people were walking across the desert. They were going to new homes in the Promised Land that God was giving them. The desert was hot and dry. There was not enough water for God's people to drink.

The good man Moses was leading God's people. He prayed to God. God told him how to get water for the people. Moses did what God told him to. He went to a big rock. He hit the rock with his walking stick. Water came rushing out.

The Bible says Jesus is like the rock that gives us water. Can you praise Him for that today?

READ AND REMEMBER PROVERBS 3:5-6

A Cup of Water

Jesus says, "Anyone who gives you a cup of water in my name because you belong to Christ will certainly not lose his reward."

MARK 9:41

Has someone ever given you a cold drink of water just when you wanted it most? Jesus wants you to be someone who gives a refreshing cold drink to others. He especially wants you to do this for anyone who believes in Him and loves Him. Do it just for Jesus. This is how you show your love for Him. You show your love for Him by doing good things for other people who belong to Jesus.

If you do these good things for them, Jesus will smile on you. And He will give you good things in heaven.

LISTEN TO JESUS IN MATTHEW 10:40-42

Water for Jesus

*Jesus says, "I was thirsty
and you gave me something to drink…"*
MATTHEW 25:35

Someday everyone will see Jesus as the
mighty King. Everyone will stand before
His throne. Then He will separate
everyone. He will put some people
on one side, and some on the other.

Jesus will have good words for the
people on one side. He will give them good rewards. He will
say, "I was thirsty, and you gave Me something to drink." They
will say, "When did we ever see You thirsty and give You
something to drink?" Jesus will answer that whenever we do
good things for anyone who belongs to Jesus, then we are
doing good things for Him.

What good things can you do for one who belongs to Jesus?

LISTEN TO JESUS IN MATTHEW 25:31-46

Thirsty Inside

The Bible says, "Whoever wishes,
let him take the free gift of the water of life."
REVELATION 22:17

Have you ever wanted so much to be close to God that it was like being thirsty inside?

Jesus promises that when we are truly thirsty inside, He will give us a drink. What He gives us will taste better than anything we have ever tasted. He will give us the water of life. He gives us this water for free. Jesus says, "Come and drink."

His water is clear and clean. There is always plenty of it. You can drink all you want, and every drink will always taste good. Are you glad that Jesus has this water for us? Talk to Jesus about this in a prayer.

READ REVELATION 21:6, 22:17

All Kinds of Trees

*The Bible says, "The Lord God made all kinds of trees…
trees that were pleasing to the eye and good for food."*
GENESIS 2:9

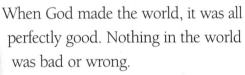

When God made the world, it was all perfectly good. Nothing in the world was bad or wrong.

Adam and Eve were the first man and woman. God let them live in a place called Eden. Many fruit trees grew there. Their fruit tasted delicious. God said Adam and Eve could eat the fruit from any of those trees — all except one. There was one tree whose fruit they were not to eat. But all the other fruit on all the other trees was theirs to eat.

Praise God that He gives us so many good things to enjoy!

READ GENESIS 1:29, 2:8-17

The Different Tree

God said, "Have you eaten from the tree
that I commanded you not to eat from?"
GENESIS 3:11

Eden was the beautiful place where
Adam and Eve lived. In the middle of
Eden were two special fruit trees. One
was called the Tree of Life. Anyone
who ate fruit from this tree would
live forever, and never die. The other
tree was different. God told Adam
and Eve not to eat any fruit from this other tree. "If you do,
you will die," God said.

But Adam and Eve disobeyed God. They ate fruit from
this other tree. As punishment, God made them leave Eden.
They could never go back and eat from the Tree of Life.

When you see fruit trees, remember what happened in Eden.

READ GENESIS 3

The Tree of Life

Jesus says, "Blessed are those who wash their robes,
that they may have the right to the tree of life..."
R E V E L A T I O N   2 2 : 1 4

Adam and Eve disobeyed God. So God chased them out of
Eden. The Tree of Life was there in Eden. God would not let
Adam and Eve eat fruit from this tree. Anyone who ate fruit
from this tree would live forever. But Adam and Eve could
not live forever. They had to die.

Someday we will see the Tree of Life.
We will see it in the middle of New
Jerusalem, the city coming down out
of heaven from God. We will see it,
and be glad. Jesus has died for us.
Now we can eat from the Tree of Life.

Praise God that we can now live
forever.

Like a Hammer

God says, "Is not my word like fire,
and like a hammer that breaks a rock in pieces?"
JEREMIAH 23:29

How many things can a hammer do? When we swing it with our hand, a hammer can push a nail into a thick piece of wood. Or a hammer can break something apart, and smash it into pieces.

The Bible is God's Word. And God says that His Word is like a hammer that can smash a rock into pieces.

Sometimes we think about bad things instead of good things. Those bad thoughts are like hard rocks in our mind. Give thanks to God that He has given us the Bible to smash those hard rocks into pieces.

READ JEREMIAH 23:29

Like a Hammer

God says, "Is not my word…
like a hammer that breaks a rock in pieces?"
JEREMIAH 23:29

God says His Word is like a hammer that can smash a rock into pieces. If you have bad thoughts in your mind, let God's Word break them up. You might think you want to do something mean or ugly to someone. But remember God's Word. The Bible says, "Be kind to one another" (Ephesians 4:32).

You might think you want to tell a lie. Then remember God's Word. The Bible says, "Do not lie" (Colossians 3:9).

You might think you want to worry and be upset about something, instead of praying. Then remember God's Word. The Bible says, "Don't be worried about anything" (Philippians 4:6).

READ 2 CORINTHIANS 10:5

Like a Hammer

God says, "Is not my word...like a hammer?"
JEREMIAH 23:29

When we have bad thoughts in our mind, God's Word can break them up. God's Word is like a hammer that can smash a rock to pieces. You may think you want to brag or boast about something. But remember God's Word, which says, "Humble yourselves before the Lord" (James 4:10).

You may think you want to be grouchy and grumpy. Then remember God's Word, which says, "Be joyful always" (1 Thessalonians 5:16).

You may think you want to complain about something, or argue with someone. Remember God's Word, which says, "Do everything without complaining or arguing" (Philippians 2:14).

READ PSALM 29:3-5

Helmet of Salvation

The Bible says, "Take the helmet of salvation…"
EPHESIANS 6:17

You and I are in a battle. Our enemy the devil is fighting against God's people. As God's good soldiers, we must fight the way our Lord tells us to fight. We must also wear the armor He gives us to wear.

God gives us a helmet to cover our head. It is called the helmet of salvation. If we want to wear it, we must remember how Jesus rescued us. Never forget how Jesus died to take away your sins. Think about how He died just for you, and just for me, and for everyone.

If you truly remember this, you will wear the helmet of salvation.

LOOK CLOSELY AT 1 TIMOTHY 1:15

Helmet of Salvation

The Bible says, "Take the helmet of salvation…"
EPHESIANS 6:17

God gives us the helmet of salvation to wear. If we remember how Jesus died to save us from our sins, we can wear this helmet.

If we wear this helmet, we will think good thoughts, not bad thoughts. We will remember how much Jesus loves us. We will remember how good and great He is. We will remember how much He loves other people. We will remember that someday we will see Jesus.

Someday He will come back for us. And we want to be ready for Him. We want to be thinking good thoughts. What good thoughts do you have right now?

READ CAREFULLY 2 CORINTHIANS 5:6-10

Helmet of Salvation

*The Bible says, "Let us put on…
the hope of salvation as a helmet."*
1 THESSALONIANS 5:8

If we put on the helmet of salvation, we will think good thoughts, not bad thoughts.

We will use the helmet of salvation to protect how we think. We will not watch bad television shows and movies. We will not listen to people who say bad words and bad jokes. We will not listen to people who always complain or argue.

Instead we will ask Jesus to be our helmet. We will ask Him to protect our mind. We will ask Him to help us think good thoughts, and not bad thoughts. Can you pray these things now?

READ AND REMEMBER PHILIPPIANS 4:8

God Grows Grain

The Bible says, "The streams of God are filled with water to provide the people with grain..."

PSALM 65:9

Do you like to eat bread, or rolls, or buns, or noodles, or biscuits, or muffins, or cereal, or bagels, or pancakes, or doughnuts, or cookies, or cake? All these foods are made from grain. God has made our world so that plenty of grain will grow. Then we can have lots of good foods like these.

God made the dirt where the grain is planted. And He sends rain to water it while it grows. He does all this for us.

So be glad, and praise God. Praise and thank Him for how well He takes care of us.

READ AND ENJOY PSALM 65:9-13

The Kingdom Grows

Jesus says, "All by itself the soil produces grain—
first the stalk, then the head, then the full kernel in the head."
MARK 4:28

When Jesus was here in the world, He helped us remember that He is our King. A king is the person who is in charge of everything. And everything he is in charge of is called his kingdom.

Jesus said that His kingdom is growing. It is growing like grain that grows out in the field. First the grain is little. Then it grows bigger. Then it grows even bigger. Someday it will be all grown up.

The kingdom of Jesus is growing. So we must be patient. Someday we will see Him as the King. We will see His crown and His throne. But first we must wait a little while. Will you be patient, and wait?

LISTEN TO JESUS IN MARK 4:26-29

Rich Toward God

God says, "I will send rain on your land in its season…
so that you may gather in your grain…"
DEUTERONOMY 11:14

Once there was a man who grew lots and lots of grain in his
fields. He became a very rich man. He could buy everything
he wanted.

One day he decided to build big barns to store his extra
grain. He decided not to work anymore. He would just have
a party all the time. He did not think at all about giving anything to God, or about giving grain to other people. So that
night God said to the rich man, "It is time
for you to die."

Always remember to be richer to
God and to others than you are to
yourself.

LISTEN TO JESUS IN LUKE 12:16-21

God's Shadow

*The Bible says, "He who dwells in the shelter of the Most High
will rest in the shadow of the Almighty."*
PSALM 91:1

Does God have a shadow? In a way, He does. God's shadow is a shadow of light and warmth. His shadow is where we can come close to Him. We are safe in God's shadow. He protects us there. We go to His shadow because we love Him.

In God's shadow we can feel His warmth and hear His voice, even when He whispers. We can rest. We know nothing can hurt us. Nothing bad can get to us.

God loves it when we come into His shadow. You can do that as you pray to Him. Will you pray to Him now?

READ PSALM 91

Peter's Shadow

The Bible says, "People brought the sick into the streets…
that Peter's shadow might fall on them as he passed by."
ACTS 5:15

The good man Peter loved Jesus. After Jesus rose from the dead and then went back to heaven, God's Holy Spirit came to live in Peter. Peter became strong. He kept telling people about Jesus.

Peter and the other friends of Jesus did many mighty miracles. They made many people well who were sick. So everyone who was sick wanted to come to Peter. Sick people wanted Peter's shadow to fall on them, and heal them that way.

A miracle is a surprising thing that only God can do. Only God can make a miracle. And sometimes He does His miracles through people like Peter, or you, or me.

READ THE STORY IN ACTS 5:12-16

Just a Shadow

The Bible says, "The law is only a shadow
of the good things that are coming…"
HEBREWS 10:1

Sometimes we see someone's shadow, but we cannot see the person. (Maybe he is behind a corner, but his shadow comes out around it.) The shadow is not the person. The shadow just has the person's shape.

Some of the things we read in the Bible are like shadows. In Jerusalem there was a building called the temple. It was where God's people worshiped Him. They called it God's house. But God's real house is in heaven. The temple was just a shadow of His real house.

Praise God that someday we will see God's real heaven, where there will not be any shadows.

READ HEBREWS 8:3-6

The Sun Stopped

The Bible says, "The sun stopped in the middle of the sky and delayed going down about a full day."
JOSHUA 10:13

One day God's soldiers were fighting a big battle against God's enemies. There were many enemies, and they were strong.

The good man Joshua was the leader of God's soldiers. God told Joshua not to be afraid of those enemies that day. The Lord promised Joshua that His soldiers would win the battle. That same day, Joshua prayed to the Lord. He prayed that the sun and moon would stand still. So the sun stopped in the middle of the sky. It did not go down until the next day. God's people had lots of time to win the battle.

Praise God for the miracle He did, when He answered Joshua's prayer.

READ THE STORY IN JOSHUA 10:7-15

Shine Like the Sun

*Jesus says, "The righteous will shine like the sun
in the kingdom of their Father."*
MATTHEW 13:43

Someday we will all see the kingdom of God. Jesus will be King. He will be in charge of everything. We will see Him wearing His crown and sitting on His throne.

Only righteous people will be with Him there forever. Who are the righteous people? They are the people Jesus has made clean. They believe in Him and love Him. "Righteous" means that they are all "right." Jesus makes them right and good.

When the day of God's kingdom comes, Jesus says we will shine as bright as the sun. Give thanks to Jesus that someday you will be so bright.

LISTEN TO JESUS IN MATTHEW 13:40-43

No Sun

The Bible says, "The city does not need the sun...
for the glory of God gives it light..."
REVELATION 21:23

Be glad that someday we will see the New Jerusalem, the city coming down out of heaven from God.

There will be no darkness there. Is that because the sun is shining all the time, and never goes down? No, there will not be any sun in the sky above that city. The sun will not even be needed there. God Himself will be the light of that city. And God is brighter than the sun. There in God's heavenly city, you will never see any darkness again.

Praise God that He is full of light, and that He will shine bright for us forever.

Riding a Donkey

The Bible says, "The donkey saw the angel of the Lord..."
NUMBERS 22:23,25,27

One day a man was riding a donkey. He was on his way to do something wrong to God's people. God was not pleased with him. God's angel came to stop him.

The donkey saw the angel, and stopped. But the man did not see the angel. He started beating his donkey. So God opened the donkey's mouth so she could talk to him. Then God opened the man's eyes so he could see the angel. Now the man finally started listening to God.

Ask God to show you when you are about to do something wrong, so you will not do it. Watch and listen carefully for God.

READ THE STORY IN NUMBERS 22:21-35

Riding a Donkey

The Bible says, "See, your king comes to you, righteous and having salvation, gentle and riding on a donkey…"
ZECHARIAH 9:9

One day a Man was riding a donkey. He was on His way to do something good for God's people. God was pleased with Him.

He was a good Man. He always did what was right and helpful. He was gentle. He was Jesus, our King. He was riding the donkey into Jerusalem, where He would be killed. He would die to take the punishment for all the wrong things we do.

As Jesus rode that donkey into Jerusalem, many people came out to cheer and shout. If you had been there, what would you have said to Him? What will you say to Him now?

READ MATTHEW 21:1-11

Riding a Donkey

Jesus said, "He put the man on his own donkey…"
LUKE 10:34

One day a man was riding a donkey. As he was on his way, he did something good for someone who needed help. And God was pleased with him.

The man saw someone lying by the road. It was someone who was badly hurt. So the man on the donkey stopped. He went over to the hurt man. He put on medicine and bandages. Then he put the hurt man on his donkey. He took him to a place where he could rest and get better.

Jesus said that we all must help other people who are hurt, just as the man on the donkey did.

READ THE STORY IN LUKE 10:25-37

The Lord's Battle

In the Bible, David says, "It is not by sword or spear
that the Lord saves; for the battle is the Lord's…"
1   S A M U E L   1 7 : 4 7

The young boy David was not afraid to fight Goliath. Goliath was one of God's enemies. He was a giant. He carried a huge, heavy spear. He also had a sword and a smaller spear.

When David went out against him, David did not have a spear or a sword. He knew he did not need these. He knew God was with him. He knew God is stronger than any weapon. He knew that God decides the winner of every battle, because God is stronger than all the world's armies. David said, "The battle is the Lord's."

Praise God that He is mighty.

READ THE STORY IN 1 SAMUEL 17:1-50

Taking a Spear

The Bible says, "David took the spear…"
1 SAMUEL 26:12

The man Saul was not obeying God. He and his soldiers were chasing the good man David. They were trying to hurt him. David had to run away.

One night Saul and his soldiers lay down on the ground to sleep. David saw them. He walked over to them. Saul did not wake up. David could have hurt him. But he did not. He just picked up Saul's spear, and took it away for a while. He gave it back later, and showed Saul that he was not trying to hurt him.

If someone tries to hurt you, be like David was that night. Do not try to hurt others.

READ 1 PETER 2:21-24

Jesus Is Speared

*The Bible says, "One of the soldiers pierced
Jesus' side with a spear..."*
JOHN 19:34

When Jesus was nailed to the cross, He hurt terribly, and kept hurting. Slowly He began to die. Once he called out, "I am thirsty." A soldier soaked a sponge in vinegar. He put the sponge on a stick, and lifted it to Jesus' lips. Jesus sucked some vinegar from the sponge.

Then Jesus said, "It is finished." He bowed His head and let Himself die. But a soldier took his spear and threw it into Jesus' body. More of Jesus' blood came out.

Never forget how much Jesus was hurt that day. Always remember that He died for you and me.

READ JOHN 19:28-37

The King's Ring

The Bible says, "Pharaoh took his signet ring…
and put it on Joseph's finger."
GENESIS 41:42

The good man Joseph was in prison. The people who put him in prison should not have done this. It was wrong. But Joseph was patient.

One night the king of Egypt had two strange dreams. God was showing the king something in these dreams. But the king did not understand. Joseph was the only person who could help the king understand those dreams. Joseph told the king what God was showing him.

The king was glad. He made Joseph his helper. And he even let Joseph wear the king's ring. Praise God that He is so good to those who wait patiently for Him.

READ GENESIS 41

The King's Ring

*The Bible says, "The king took off his signet ring...
and presented it to Mordecai."*
ESTHER 8:2

In the Bible, a good man named Mordecai was the uncle of a good woman named Esther. Mordecai and Esther were a part of God's people. But there was a bad man who hated Mordecai. He was trying to get all of God's people killed.

What could Mordecai and Esther do? Mordecai helped Esther be brave. Esther went politely to the king. She told the king what the bad man was trying to do. So the king protected God's people. He made Mordecai his helper. And he even let Mordecai wear the king's ring.

Praise God that He is so great and good to His people.

READ ESTHER 8

The King's Ring

*God said, "I will make you like my signet ring,
for I have chosen you…"*
HAGGAI 2:23

In the Bible, God gave His people the Promised Land where they could live. But they did not always love God there and obey Him. God waited patiently. But finally the time came when He punished them by making them leave the Promised Land. They had to be gone a long time. Finally God let them come back.

In those days, the king of God's people was named Zerubbabel. God promised him that he would be like God's royal ring. God promised to help Him.

Praise God that He is our King. Since we are His children, we are His royal family. We are like His royal ring.

READ HAGGAI 2:20-23

Dry Bones

The Bible says, "Dry bones, hear the word of the Lord!"
EZEKIEL 37:4

In the Bible, the Holy Spirit took the good man Ezekiel to a valley. The valley was full of bones that were dry. God decided to make the bones come alive. He told Ezekiel to speak to the bones, and tell them what God was going to do.

Ezekiel talked to the bones. They started shaking and rattling. The bones came together. Suddenly they had muscles and skin. Then Ezekiel talked to them again. This time the wind blew, and there was breath in these new bodies. Now they were alive.

Praise God and thank Him that He can take what is dead and make it become alive.

READ THE STORY IN EZEKIEL 37:1-14

Adam's Bone

*In the Bible, Adam says, "This is now bone of my bones
and flesh of my flesh; she shall be called Woman…"*
GENESIS 2:23

When God made the first people, at first He made only
a man. God made Adam
from the dust of the
ground.

Adam lived in Eden. No other people were there. Adam
had no helper. He was alone. Then God said, "It is not good
for him to be alone. I will make the right helper for him."
God made Adam go to sleep. God took a bone from inside
Adam. From this bone, God made a woman. Then Adam
woke up. God brought the woman to him.

Give thanks and praise to God that He has made both
man and woman.

READ THE STORY IN GENESIS 2:18-24

Dead Bones

Jesus said, "You are like whitewashed tombs, which look beautiful on the outside but on the inside are full of dead men's bones."
MATTHEW 23:27

In the days when Jesus lived in the Promised Land, some men were there who were called Pharisees. They were not kind or fair or loving. They were not humble. They were proud. They wanted everyone to see them and say hello to them. They wanted everyone to notice how good they were. They prayed in loud voices so other people could hear them.

Jesus told them they were like tombs painted white. They looked good on the outside. But inside they were full of dead bones and dirt.

Ask God to keep you clean on the inside, where it matters most.

LISTEN TO JESUS IN MATTHEW 23:25-28

Through the Gates

The Bible says, "Enter his gates with thanksgiving…"
PSALM 100:4

In the old days, cities had big, thick walls around them. To go in and out of the city, you had to go through big gates, which were like doors in the walls.

Jerusalem had walls around it, and there were gates in the walls. People who came to Jerusalem to worship God could walk through those gates. The people sang songs of praise to God as they came through the gates. They gave thanks to God.

You can come to God anywhere, and at any time, to praise and worship Him. So be glad, and give Him thanks.

READ AND ENJOY PSALM 100

Outside the Gates

The Bible says, "Jesus also suffered outside the city gate…"
HEBREWS 13:12

The soldiers in Jerusalem took Jesus to kill Him on the cross. They took Him through the gates to a place outside the city walls.

This was the place where Jesus died for you and me. He died to take away our sins. When our sins are taken away, then we are clean inside. Jesus loves us, and He wants us to be clean inside. That is why He died.

So let's remember every day to thank God for sending Jesus to die for us. Call out the name of Jesus every day, and praise Him.

READ HEBREWS 13:11-16

Twelve Gates

The Bible says, "The city had a great, high wall with twelve gates, and with twelve angels at the gates."
REVELATION 21:12

Praise God that we will someday see the New Jerusalem coming down out of heaven from God. The city walls will be covered with beautiful gems and jewels. The walls will have twelve gates. Each gate will be made from a huge pearl.

The gates will always be open. God's people will all come inside. Everyone who believes in Jesus, and loves Jesus, and belongs to Jesus will come gladly through the gates.

Praise God for these gates and walls. Praise Him for this beautiful city that will be our home forever. Be glad in the Lord always. I will say it again: Be glad!

READ REVELATION 21:12-21

Better than Gold

The Bible says, "The ordinances of the Lord…
are more precious than gold, than much pure gold…"
PSALM 19:9-10

When the fall of the year comes, many leaves on the trees turn gold. Isn't it a beautiful color? Gold is always so beautiful. Rings and necklaces and bracelets and watchbands are often made of the metal gold. Anything gold will cost a lot of money. Everyone likes gold.

The Bible says there is something far better than gold. God's words are more precious than gold. It is better to hear and know God's words than to have a whole house full of gold. Do you want to know God's words more than you want anything made of gold?

READ PSALM 19:7-11

Clean Gold

The Bible say that "your faith" is "of greater worth than gold…"
1 PETER 1:7

Gold is the one metal in all the world that people love most. Gold is very heavy. If you put gold with other metals in a very hot fire, the fire will float away the other metals, but not the gold. The gold that is left is clean and strong.

The Bible says our faith is like gold. Faith means believing in God. Sometimes we go through some troubles. These troubles will show how clean and strong our faith is.

Are you going through any troubles? If you are, tell God "Thank You" that He is making your faith clean and strong.

LOOK CAREFULLY AT 1 PETER 1:6-9

City of Gold

The Bible says, "The city was made of pure gold, as pure as glass."
REVELATION 21:18

The New Jerusalem — the city coming down out of heaven from God — is made of pure gold. The biggest street is made of gold. Just imagine a wide, long street all golden as far as you can see. That is more gold than anyone has ever seen.

God's holy city in heaven will be richer and finer and bigger and more beautiful than anything we have ever seen in this world. But all this is not what you will love most there. What you will love most is always getting to be with God.

In a prayer, tell God how much you will enjoy being with Him.

Smoking Mountain

*The Bible says, "When the people saw…
the mountain in smoke, they trembled with fear."*
EXODUS 20:18

The people of God were going to their new homes in the Promised Land. Moses was their leader. Soon they came to a high mountain called Sinai. The Lord asked Moses to come up the mountain so He could speak with Moses.

There were clouds and thunder and lightning on the mountain. There was also more smoke than you or I have ever seen. Smoke comes from fire. There was so much smoke on the mountain because God's fire was on the mountain. God is powerful and bright. He is stronger and hotter and brighter than any fire you and I have ever seen.

Next time you see smoke, remember God's awesome fire.

READ EXODUS 19:16-19

Smoking Temple

The Bible says, "The temple was filled with smoke."
ISAIAH 6:4

God let the good man Isaiah look into heaven. Isaiah saw the Lord seated on His throne in His temple in heaven. Isaiah heard angels saying to one another, "Holy, holy, holy is the Lord Almighty." They also said, "The whole earth is full of God's glory."

When they said this, everything shook like an earthquake. Isaiah saw the temple fill up with smoke.

Smoke comes from fire. The glory of God is like a fire, and makes smoke. Remember God the next time you see smoke. Give praise to Him for His awesome glory.

LOOK AT REVELATION 15:8

As Smoke Dissapears

The Bible says, "The heavens will vanish like smoke..."
ISAIAH 51:6

After smoke rises up in the sky, where does it go? Where has all the smoke gone from all the fires that the world has seen?

After a while, smoke just disappears. It vanishes. It goes away. The Bible says that this is what will happen someday to the sky. The sky we see now will disappear. It will vanish. It will all go away — sun, moon, stars, and clouds and blue and gray. Then we will see everything new, including a new sky.

Tell God "Thank You" for the sky He has given us to enjoy a little while longer.

READ JOEL 2:28-32

Made of Wood

God said to Noah, "Make yourself an ark of wood…"
GENESIS 6:14

Wood comes from trees. When Noah built the ark, he made it from wood. He must have had to cut many trees to get enough wood. The ark was a very big boat.

This ark, made of wood, kept Noah and his family and the animals safe during the great flood. They did not have to die. God made a way for them to live.

The cross Jesus died on was also made of wood. The cross is what keeps you and me and all of God's people safe. Through the cross, God lets us live forever. Tell God "Thank You" that Jesus died on the cross of wood.

READ 1 PETER 2:24

From Bitter to Sweet

*The Bible says, "Moses cried out to the Lord,
and the Lord showed him a piece of wood."*
EXODUS 15:25

God's people were walking across the desert. The desert was hot. The people were tired and thirsty. They came to a place with a pool of water. But the water was bitter. It tasted awful. The people could not drink it. "What will we drink?" the people asked Moses.

Moses was their leader. Moses prayed to the Lord. The Lord showed Moses a piece of wood. Moses picked it up and threw it in the water. Suddenly the water became sweet and good.

God can take whatever is bitter, and make it sweet. Tell God "Thank You" that He can always do this.

READ THE STORY IN EXODUS 15:22-27

Wood for the Temple

In the Bible, David says, "I have taken great pains to provide
for the temple of the Lord…quantities of wood and stone."
1 CHRONICLES 22:14

In Jerusalem, God's people built a beautiful building called
the temple. It was a place where they could worship God.
God told the good man David how to make the temple.
David told Solomon. Then Solomon built the temple.

There was plenty of strong, beautiful wood in the temple.
It smelled good, too. Most of it was cedar wood. Have you
smelled cedar wood before?

Everything about the temple was
good and strong and beautiful. Give praise to our
God that He loves what
is good and strong and
beautiful.

READ 2 CHRONICLES 2:3-16

The Wolf Attacks

Jesus says, "The wolf attacks the flock and scatters it."
JOHN 10:12

A wolf is a dangerous animal around sheep. Wolves eat sheep. A wolf will go after whatever sheep he wants. What should a shepherd do when a wolf attacks his sheep? A good shepherd will fight the wolf. He would rather get hurt by the wolf than have one of his sheep eaten up. But a shepherd who isn't good will run away if a wolf comes. He does not care about the sheep.

We are like sheep. Jesus is our Good Shepherd. He protects us. He fights the wolf for us. Give praise and thanks to Jesus that He lays down His life for the sheep.

LISTEN TO JESUS IN JOHN 10:11-15

Wrong Teachers

Jesus says, "I am sending you out like sheep among wolves."
MATTHEW 10:16

We are like sheep in God's pasture. Jesus says there are many wolves who will try to attack us. Who are they?

These wolves are people who try to teach us wrong things about God, and about Jesus the Son of God, and about God's Holy Spirit. These wrong teachers do not really believe in Jesus and love Him and belong to Him. They do not obey God. They do not have God's Holy Spirit inside them. Jesus tells us to watch out for them.

Ask God to protect you from these wrong teachers. Ask Him to show you what is right and true.

READ PAUL'S WARNING IN ACTS 20:29-31

Wolf with the Lamb

The Bible says, "The wolf will live with the lamb…"
ISAIAH 11:6

A day is coming when wolves and lambs will lie down together in peace. A calf and a lion will lie down together. The cow and the bear will eat together. And a little child will lead these animals from place to place. Animals will never again hurt one another, or hurt people, either.

When will this day come? It will come when the kingdom of Jesus is all grown up. When you see Jesus and His crown and His throne, then you can go and play with the biggest and wildest animal you want to.

You can thank God now, even before it happens.

READ AND ENJOY ISAIAH 11:1-9

The Dragon Fights

*The Bible says, "Michael and his angels fought against the dragon,
and the dragon and his angels fought back."*
REVELATION 12:7

Jesus spoke to the good man John from heaven. Jesus showed John many things in heaven. John also saw things that have happened in this world, and things that will happen later.

John saw a huge dragon. The dragon is our enemy, Satan. There was war in heaven. Satan the dragon and his army were fighting against God's angels. But God's angels are stronger than Satan's army. So Satan and his army were thrown away from heaven. They can never go back.

Give thanks and praise to God that He and His angels are stronger than Satan.

LISTEN TO JESUS IN LUKE 10:17-18

The Dragon Loses

*The Bible says, "The great dragon was hurled down—
that ancient serpent called the devil, or Satan…"*
REVELATION 12:9

Jesus showed the good man John many things. Jesus showed John what would happen to Satan. John saw a huge dragon. The dragon is our enemy, Satan. Satan tried to fight against Jesus. But Jesus is already the Winner over Satan. Jesus has defeated Satan. When did Jesus win against Satan?

Jesus won when He died on the cross and when He rose from the dead, and when He went back to heaven to be with God. Satan still tries to fight against people who believe in Jesus and love Jesus. But that will be over someday soon.

Praise Jesus now that He has won against Satan!

READ HEBREWS 2:14-15

The Dragon Dies

The Bible says, "An angel seized the dragon, that ancient serpent, who is the devil, or Satan, and bound him for a thousand years."
REVELATION 20:2

Jesus showed the good man John what will happen to Satan. John saw a huge, angry dragon. The dragon is our enemy, Satan. Someday an angel will come from heaven. The angel will capture Satan. He will put chains around the dragon and throw him in prison.

Satan will be there for a long time. Later he will come out again for just a short while. But God will send fire down from heaven against him. God will throw Satan into a lake of fire. Satan will be punished forever.

So be glad, and praise God. Praise and thank Him that He will destroy Satan forever.

READ REVELATION 20:1-10

Living with Pigs

The Bible says, "He longed to fill his stomach
with the pods that the pigs were eating."
L U K E   1 5 : 1 6

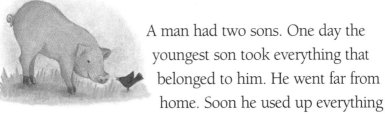

A man had two sons. One day the youngest son took everything that belonged to him. He went far from home. Soon he used up everything he owned. He had nothing to eat. He lived with pigs.

Now he knew that he had been wrong. He decided to go back and say to his father, "I was wrong." The father saw him coming back. He ran out and hugged and kissed his son. He gave him new clothes and a party. The father was so glad.

Whenever we have done something bad, God is so glad when we come back to Him and say, "I was wrong."

READ THE STORY IN LUKE 15:11-24

Demons and Pigs

The Bible says, "A large herd of pigs was feeding on the nearby hillside."
MARK 5:11

One day Jesus came to a place by the Sea of Galilee. A man there was hurting. Satan's demons lived inside him. They made him cut himself with rocks. When Jesus came, the bad demons were afraid. They knew Jesus is good and strong. They knew He would make them stop hurting that man.

On a hill by the sea, the demons saw some pigs. They begged Jesus to let them go into the pigs. So Jesus let them. This made the pigs run down the hill into the sea. All the pigs drowned.

Give thanks to Jesus that He protects us from Satan's demons.

READ THE STORY IN MARK 5:1-13

Tell Your Family

*The Bible says, "The evil spirits came out
and went into the pigs."*
MARK 5:13

Jesus helped a man who was
being hurt by Satan's demons.
Jesus made the demons leave the
man. The demons went into some
pigs. The pigs ran into the sea and drowned.

The man Jesus helped was now so much better. The demons
did not hurt him anymore. He did not cut himself with rocks
anymore. The man was glad. Now he wanted to go and be
with Jesus. But Jesus said, "Go home to your family. Tell them
how much the Lord has done for you. Tell them the good
things He did for you." So the man did this.

What has the Lord done for you? Who can you tell this to?

READ THE STORY IN MARK 5:14-20

A Sharp Sword

The Bible says, "The word of God is living and active,
sharper than any double-edged sword…"
HEBREWS 4:12

God does not stay quiet. God speaks to us in the Bible. In the Bible we can read and hear God's Word. God's Word is alive and working, because God is alive and working. The Bible says that God's Word is like a sword. It is sharp. It cuts through all the way inside us. It can find everything inside us. If we have wrong thoughts, God's Word goes inside us and finds them. We will see those wrong thoughts. We will see how wrong they are.

Then we can go to God and admit where we have been wrong. He will forgive us, because Jesus died for those sins.

READ CAREFULLY HEBREWS 4:12-16

Sword of the Spirit

The Bible says, "Take…the sword of the Spirit, which is the word of God."
EPHESIANS 6:17

God's Holy Spirit carries a sword. God's Holy Spirit carries this weapon as He comes to live inside us. This is the weapon He shares with us as we fight against God's enemy, Satan.

The sword of God's Spirit is the Word of God. God's Word is the sword we must use when Satan attacks us. If wrong thoughts come into our mind and heart, we must use the sword of God's Word to kill those wrong thoughts.

God's Holy Spirit will help us use this sword every time we need it. So be glad, and praise the Holy Spirit. Give thanks to God's Spirit for His sword.

READ CAREFULLY EPHESIANS 6:10-18

A Sharp Sword

The Bible says, "Out of his mouth comes a sharp sword with which to strike down the nations."
REVELATION 19:15

God let the good man John look up into heaven. John saw Jesus riding a white horse. His eyes were like fire. The armies of God's angels were following Him. And out of His mouth came a sharp sword.

Jesus will use that sword to cut down all the people who will not believe in Him and love Him and obey Him. Every word Jesus says will be like a sharp sword. Every word He says will cut and sting. Every word He says will hurt His enemies who hate Him and will not do what He says.

Praise Jesus that His every word is strong and powerful.

READ REVELATION 19:11-21

A Scarlet Robe

The Bible says, "They stripped him and put a scarlet robe on him…"
MATTHEW 27:28

Jesus was captured. Soldiers in Jerusalem beat Him and made fun of Him. They took off His clothes. They put a bright-colored robe on Him. On His head they put a crown of thorns they had made. They bowed down and laughed and said, "Hail, King of the Jews!" They spat on Him, and slapped Him. Then they took Him away to kill Him on the cross.

But no one will ever do that to Jesus again. Jesus really is the King. He is with God at His throne in heaven.

Think about Jesus now. Praise Him that He is your King.

READ AND REMEMBER HEBREWS 12:2-3

Maker of Robes

*The Bible says, "The widows stood around him, crying
and showing him the robes and other clothing Dorcas had made…"*
ACTS 9:39

In the Bible, a good woman named Dorcas was always doing
good things and helping people who were poor. Dorcas knew
how to make clothes. She made robes and other clothes for
many of her friends. But Dorcas became sick. One day she died.
Her friends washed her body and laid it in an upstairs room.

Then the good man Peter came there. He went upstairs.
Dorcas's friends were there crying. They showed
Peter the robes Dorcas had made. Peter knelt down
and talked to Jesus. Then he told the dead woman
to get up. Dorcas opened her eyes, and sat up.
Peter helped her stand. She was alive!

Give praise to Jesus that He can
make the dead come back to life.

READ THE STORY IN ACTS 9:36-43

White Robes

The Bible says, "They were wearing white robes…"
REVELATION 7:9

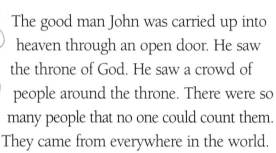

The good man John was carried up into heaven through an open door. He saw the throne of God. He saw a crowd of people around the throne. There were so many people that no one could count them. They came from everywhere in the world. They had every color of skin that people can have. All these people had washed their robes. They had washed them in the blood of Jesus, the Lamb of God. The blood of Jesus made their robes white.

Give praise to Jesus that His blood washes away our sins. His blood makes us clean and bright!

READ REVELATION 7:9-17

On Eagles' Wings

God says, "I carried you on eagles' wings
and brought you to myself."
EXODUS 19:4

Long ago, God's people were not living in the Promised Land. Instead
they were slaves and prisoners in
Egypt. The king of Egypt was
mean to them there.

But God did not forget them. He
brought them all out of Egypt. He did many miracles for them.
He showed them how awesome He is. For God's people, this
was like riding on the wings of an eagle. It was like flying
through the sky, flying all the way up to heaven.

This was what it was like when God saved them. Give
praise to God that He has saved you, and that you are as free
as an eagle.

READ EXODUS 19:3-6

On Eagles' Wings

The Bible says, "Those who hope in the Lord...
will soar on wings like eagles..."
ISAIAH 40:31

What is the tiredest you have ever been? We all get tired sometimes. Even strong young men and women get tired. All of God's people get tired.

But God never gets tired. He knows how to help all of us when we are tired. He knows how to make us strong.

Sometimes we get tired while we are doing the work God gives us. God can make us strong again. If we believe in Him, and love Him, and ask for His help, He will make us strong. We will feel as if we are flying like eagles.

READ AND ENJOY ISAIAH 40:28-31

Eagle in the Sky

*In the Bible, John says, "I heard an eagle
that was flying in midair..."*
REVELATION 8:13

When the good man John was carried up through the doorway into heaven, he saw many things.

Once he saw seven angels with seven trumpets. When they blew their trumpets, God's punishment came down. A fire storm came to the world. A burning mountain was thrown into the ocean. A burning star fell on the rivers. Darkness came to the sun and the moon and many of the stars. Then John saw a flying eagle. The eagle shouted and warned everyone that more punishment was coming.

Give praise to Jesus that He has saved you from the punishment that is coming on all the world.

READ REVELATION 8

At the Lord's Feet

The Bible says, "Mary sat at the Lord's feet
listening to what he said."
LUKE 10:39

Mary and Martha were sisters. They were Jesus' friends. One day Jesus came to visit them. He came to teach them. It was time for them to listen.

Mary sat down beside the feet of Jesus. She listened carefully. She knew how good His words are. She wanted to enjoy them and believe them. But Martha kept thinking about other things. She got busy cleaning the house and making dinner. She said, "Lord, tell Mary to help me." But Jesus was glad that Mary was listening to Him. He let her keep doing it.

Always remember how good it is to listen to Jesus.

READ THE STORY IN LUKE 10:38-42

Washing Feet

*The Bible says, "Jesus poured water into a basin
and began to wash his disciples' feet..."*
JOHN 13:5

Jesus and His friends — the twelve disciples — were having
dinner. In those days, at a dinner like that, people would
have a servant with them. Before they ate, the servant would
take off their sandals and wash everyone's feet. But tonight
no servants were there. None of the disciples wanted to
wash everyone's feet. They did not want to be a servant.

So Jesus got up from the table. He brought water and
a towel. He went around the room and washed
everyone's feet. He was their servant.

You will be like Jesus if you are a servant to
other people. What can you do now to
help someone else?

READ THE STORY IN JOHN 13:1-17

On Our Feet

The Bible says, "You will go on your way in safety,
and your foot will not stumble…"
PROVERBS 3:23

When we follow Jesus, we use our feet. Sometimes we walk. Sometimes we run. We use our feet to go help others and serve others. We use our feet to go tell others about Jesus.

The Lord keeps our feet from stumbling. He keeps our feet from getting caught in a trap. He keeps our feet on the right path. He shows us where to go and what to do. He shows us step by step.

Where does Jesus want you to go next with your feet? What is the next step He wants you to take? Ask Him to show you.

READ PROVERBS 4:11-12

The Big Dinner

*Jesus says, "A certain man was preparing a great banquet
and invited many guests..."*

LUKE 14:16

A man once prepared a big and
wonderful dinner at his house. He
invited many people to come.
Then the man sent a servant to
tell everyone the food was ready.
But everyone kept saying, "I can-
not come." They decided they wanted to do something else.

This big dinner is like all the wonderful things God will
give us in heaven. He invites everyone in the world to come
and enjoy these things. But so many people say, "I cannot come."

If you believe in Jesus and love Him, Jesus will make sure
you are there. Tell Him you are glad you have been invited.

LISTEN TO JESUS IN LUKE 14:1-24

Levi's Dinner

The Bible says, "Levi held a great banquet for Jesus at his house…"
LUKE 5:29

A man named Levi (he was also called Matthew) was sitting at a booth. People had to come there and give Levi lots of money. This money was called "taxes." People did not like to pay taxes. So they did not like Levi either.

But Jesus saw Levi, and He said, "Follow Me. Go where I go, and stay where I stay." Levi wanted to be with Jesus. He got up and left his booth. He did not take tax money from people anymore. Then Levi gave a big dinner for Jesus at his house.

What can you do for Jesus now?

READ THE STORY IN LUKE 5:27-32

The Big Dinner

The Bible says, "On this mountain the Lord Almighty will prepare a feast of rich food for all peoples..."
ISAIAH 25:6

Someday God will prepare a big dinner for the world's people. The best food you will ever taste will be there. The best meat will be there, the best drinks, and the best of everything else.

God will serve this dinner on a mountain. On that same mountain He will destroy death. No one will ever die again. God will also wipe away the tears from everyone's faces.

We will all be glad that He is our God, and that we believed in Him, and waited for Him, and asked for His help. So remember today to pray to Him, and thank Him.

READ AND ENJOY ISAIAH 25:6-9

A Blazing Torch

The Bible says, "A smoking firepot
with a blazing torch appeared..."
GENESIS 15:17

After God made many promises to Abraham, He asked Abraham to bring Him a cow, a goat, a ram, a dove, and a pigeon. Abraham was to give these animals to God. So Abraham brought the animals. He set them before God. Then Abraham fell into a deep sleep. Everything was dark. Abraham heard God's voice. He saw a torch with fire and smoke. The torch passed over the animals Abraham had given to God.

Abraham saw that God is like fire. Abraham knew that God will do what He promises to do.

Give thanks to God that He keeps His promises.

READ THE STORY IN GENESIS 15

Torches Held High

The Bible says, "Grasping the torches…they shouted,
A sword for the Lord and for Gideon!"

J U D G E S   7 : 2 0

God's people were living in the Promised Land. But their enemies kept attacking them and hurting them. One day God's angel came to the man Gideon. He told Gideon to fight their enemies and send them away.

So Gideon and his soldiers went out one night. They carried trumpets and torches. They were strong and brave. They found the place where their enemies were sleeping. They blew on their trumpets and let their torches shine high. This made their enemies afraid. Their enemies ran away.

Praise God that He makes His people strong and brave. Are you strong and brave for God?

READ THE STORY IN JUDGES 7:9-25

Torches and Weapons

*The Bible says, "Judas came…guiding soldiers….
They were carrying torches, lanterns and weapons."*
JOHN 18:3

Jesus was praying. He was in a garden where olive trees grew. Most of His twelve disciples were there. But Judas was gone. Where was he?

Judas was with the enemies of Jesus. They wanted to find Jesus. Judas decided to show them where Jesus was. He went to the garden. Soldiers went with him. They carried torches and weapons. They captured Jesus and took Him away.

What Judas did was wrong. He did not believe in Jesus or love Him or belong to Him. No, Judas did what the devil told him to do. Ask God to protect you from the devil, so that you will always love Jesus.

READ THE STORY IN MATTHEW 26:47-56

Building with Bricks

The Bible says, "They used brick instead of stone…"
GENESIS 11:3

After the great flood, Noah and his family left the ark. Their children had more children. Soon there were lots more people in the world. Then these people moved to a new place. They became proud and boastful. They carefully made lots of bricks. They began building a new city, and a high tower that would reach far up into the sky.

God did not want them to do this. So He changed the way they all talked. They could not understand each other. They could not work together. So they stopped building the city. They all moved to other places.

Give praise to God that He can do anything.

READ THE STORY IN GENESIS 11:1-9

Making Bricks

The Bible says, "They made their lives bitter
with hard labor in brick and mortar…"
EXODUS 1:14

God's people were living in Egypt. They were slaves and prisoners there. The king of Egypt was mean to them. He made them work hard all the time, without enough rest. He put them to work making bricks. They made the bricks from mud and straw.

The king of Egypt also tried to kill all the baby boys who were born to God's people. But God was kind to His people, and He did not let this happen.

Sometimes God's people must go through troubles. But give praise to God that He always watches over them.

READ THE STORY IN EXODUS 1

Making Bricks

In the Bible, Pharaoh said, "You are no longer to supply the people with straw for making bricks…"
EXODUS 5:7

God sent the good man Moses to Egypt to help His people. God wanted Moses to lead His people out of Egypt, and take them to the Promised Land. But the king of Egypt was angry when Moses came. He made the people work even harder at making bricks. God's people were hurt.

Then God did many awesome miracles in Egypt. He showed everyone how strong He is. He rescued His people out of Egypt. They did not have to be slaves anymore.

Praise God that He is awesome and strong, and can always rescue His people.

READ THE STORY IN EXODUS 5:1-6:8

The Strong Tower

The Bible says, "The name of the Lord is a strong tower;
the righteous run to it and are safe."
PROVERBS 18:10

Everything about our Lord is strong. Even His name is strong.

The Bible says His name is like a strong tower. The righteous can run inside that tower and be safe. Who are the righteous? The righteous are God's people who believe in Jesus and love Him and belong to Him. They are righteous because the Lord Jesus makes them right and good. He died for their sins, so they do not have to be wrong and bad anymore.

Whenever you are in trouble, say the name of Jesus out loud. Pray to Him. His name is a strong tower. In His name, you are safe.

READ CAREFULLY 1 JOHN 5:13-15

The Strong Tower

*In the Bible, David prays, "You have been my refuge,
a strong tower against the foe."*
PSALM 61:3

The good man David once sang a song about a tower. His song is in our Bible, and we call it as Psalm 61. David was the man God chose to be king over His people. But now David was tired and weak. He called out loud to God. He remembered how God had been like a strong tower to him. He asked God once again to take him to that strong, high tower made of rock.

David asked God to protect him with His love. And David promised to sing praise to God every day. Can you make this promise too?

HEAR DAVID'S SONG IN PSALM 61

Building a Tower

Jesus says, "Suppose one of you wants to build a tower.
Will he not first sit down and estimate the cost?"

LUKE 14:28

Do you want to follow Jesus? Do you want to always be with Him and learn from Him? Do you want to be His helper as He does awesome miracles to help other people?

If you want all this, remember that you cannot be selfish. You must let Jesus be the Owner of everything you have. You must be willing to give away whatever He asks you to.

Jesus said that if someone wants to build a tower, he must first understand how much it will cost. It is the same if you want to follow Jesus. Do you understand how much it will cost?

LISTEN TO JESUS IN LUKE 14:28-35

A Ram for God

The Bible says, "Abraham looked up…
he saw a ram caught by its horns."
GENESIS 22:13

Abraham learned how not to be selfish. He learned that God owned everything he had.

When Abraham was old, God gave him a son. Abraham named him Isaac, and loved him. But when Isaac was older, God asked Abraham to give Isaac back. God told Abraham how to do this. Abraham obeyed. He took Isaac to the top of a mountain to give him back. Abraham showed that he was not selfish. So God let Abraham keep Isaac. God showed Abraham a ram. God took the ram from Abraham instead of Isaac.

Have you been selfish about anything? Is there something God wants you to give up?

READ THE STORY IN GENESIS 22:1-19

Ram's Horn

The Bible says, "Make music to the Lord…
with the blast of the ram's horn…"
PSALM 98:5-6

God's people sang a new song. Their song is in our Bible. We call it Psalm 98. They sang the song while someone blew on a horn. The horn came from the head of a ram.

In their song they praised God because He saved them. He showed the world how good and right He is. He never forgot how much He loved His people.

They asked all the people and animals in the world to sing the song too. They asked the mountains and the ocean to sing. They asked the rivers to clap their hands. Praising God is for everyone and everything. Can you do it too?

READ AND ENJOY PSALM 98

Skipping Like Rams

The Bible says, "The mountains skipped like rams..."
PSALM 114:4

God did mighty miracles when he brought His people out of Egypt and into the Promised Land. God's people came to the Red Sea. It was big and wide and deep. But God made the waters split apart. His people walked across on dry land.

Later they came to the Jordan River. It was too wide for people to cross. So God made the waters split apart. God's people walked across on dry land.

God also made the mountains shake and quake. They were like a young ram that jumps and skips.

Give thanks to God that He shows His mighty power when He saves His people.

READ AND ENJOY PSALM 114

Through the Roof

*The Bible says, "They made an opening in the roof...
and lowered the mat the paralyzed man was lying on."*
MARK 2:4

One day Jesus was in a house crowded with people. He was teaching them about God. Some men in that town had a friend who could not walk. They wanted Jesus to heal him. They came to the house. They could not get inside because too many people were there.

So they carried the man up on the roof. They made a hole in the roof. They lowered the man down through the hole.

Jesus was glad to see what they did. He told the sick man that his sins were forgiven. He also healed him. The man stood up and walked. Everyone praised God when they saw what Jesus did. Can you praise Him now too?

READ THE STORY IN MARK 2:1-12

Alone on a Roof

A man in the Bible says, "I lie awake;
I have become like a bird alone on a roof."
PSALM 102:7

There was once a sick man who prayed to God. His prayer is in our Bible. We call it Psalm 102.

This man could not eat. He could not rest. When everyone else was sleeping, he stayed awake. He said he felt like a bird sitting alone on a roof. (Have you ever seen a bird sitting alone on a roof?)

This man told God how much he hurt. But he also praised God. He said he knew that God would be kind to His people, and help His people. The next time you are sick or hurting, remember to praise God.

READ PSALM 102

Shout from the Roof

Jesus says, "What is whispered in your ear,
proclaim from the roofs."
MATTHEW 10:27

There are many people today who do not like to hear the truth
about Jesus and about God. But Jesus says we must not be
afraid of them. We must go ahead and speak the truth. We
should say out loud what Jesus has taught us. When He tells
us something at night, we can say it out loud the next day.

He may whisper something to us in our rooms. Jesus says
we can then go up on our roofs and shout it out to everyone.

What has Jesus done for us?
What can we say out loud
about this to other people?
Who can you tell this to?

LISTEN TO JESUS IN MATTHEW 10:26-27

Jeremiah's Scroll

God said to Jeremiah, "Take a scroll
and write on it all the words I have spoken to you…"
JEREMIAH 36:2

The good man Jeremiah always told people God's words. One day God asked Jeremiah to write down those words on a scroll. Jeremiah did this. Then some men borrowed the scroll. They took it to the king. They read the words out loud. But the king did not like this. He threw the scroll in the fire. It burned up.

God told Jeremiah to take a new scroll and write down His words again. Jeremiah did this. Today we can still read these words in our Bible. Give thanks to God for giving us His Word.

READ THE STORY IN JEREMIAH 36

Jesus Reads

The Bible says, "The scroll of the prophet Isaiah was handed to Jesus."

LUKE 4:17

One day Jesus went to a place where God's people worshiped Him. The people handed Jesus a scroll with God's words on it.

Jesus stood and read from the scroll. The words He read were about Him! He said, "God's Spirit is on Me. God sent Me to tell good news to poor people. God sent Me to set prisoners free. God sent Me to make blind people see. God sent Me to help people who are hurting. God sent Me to say that now is the time when God shows you good things."

Give praise to God that He gave us the Bible to tell us about Jesus.

READ THE STORY IN LUKE 4:14-21

The Scroll in Heaven

In the Bible, John says, "I wept and wept
because no one was found who was worthy to open the scroll..."

REVELATION 5:4

When the Holy Spirit carried John into heaven, John saw God on His throne. God was holding a special scroll. It was rolled up tight.

John heard a mighty angel say, "Who is good enough to open this scroll?" Many good angels were there. But none of them was good enough to open the scroll. Many people were on the earth. But none of them was good enough to open the scroll. So John cried.

But then John saw Jesus, the Lamb of God. Jesus is good enough to do anything. Jesus opened the scroll. Give praise to Jesus that He is good enough to do anything.

READ THE STORY IN REVELATION 5

God Is a Fire

The Bible says, "Our God is a consuming fire."
HEBREWS 12:29

Our God is like a fire that can burn up everything. When God shows Himself to His people, He shows Himself in fire.

God showed Himself to Abraham as a burning torch. He showed Himself to Moses in a burning bush. He showed Himself to His people as a cloud of fire, showing them the way to the Promised Land. He showed Himself on Mount Sinai as fire and smoke and lightning and thunder, when He gave the Ten Commandments to Moses.

The next time you see fire, give praise to God that He is a fire that can burn up everything.

READ NUMBERS 11:1-3

God Is a Fire

Jesus says, "I have come to bring fire on the earth…"
LUKE 12:49

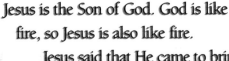

Jesus is the Son of God. God is like fire, so Jesus is also like fire.

Jesus said that He came to bring fire on the earth. The fire of Jesus will clean us and make us better and stronger. It will burn away what is weak and wrong inside us. Jesus baptizes and cleans us with fire.

When Jesus comes again to the world as our mighty King, His eyes will burn with fire.

The next time you see fire, give praise to Jesus that He is a fire that can burn up everything.

READ LUKE 3:16-17

God Is a Fire

The Bible says, "Do not put out the Spirit's fire…."
1 THESSALONIANS 5:19

God's Holy Spirit is a fire. Jesus sends the Holy Spirit to live inside us. We must not put out the Spirit's fire.

The Holy Spirit's fire inside us is like a candle flame. It can be a warm and quiet light that helps us understand God's Word. It is a true and steady light that shows us what we must do. It is a burning light that shows us whatever wrong thoughts we have.

The next time you see fire, praise God and thank Him for the Holy Spirit. And do not put out the Spirit's fire.

READ ACTS 2:1-4

The Hand of God

The Bible says, "The hand of the Lord is powerful"
JOSHUA 4:24

The Bible says that the Lord's hand is strong (Deuteronomy 3:24). The Lord's hand is mighty (Deuteronomy 7:19). God carries His holy people in His hands (Deuteronomy 33:3). There are good things forever at God's right hand (Psalm 16:11). God rescues His people with His right hand (Psalm 17:7). God's hand will capture His enemies (Psalm 21:8). All of our time is in God's hands (Psalm 31:15). If a good man stumbles, God's hands will keep Him from falling (Psalm 37:24).

Look at your hands, and remember God's hands. Tell God "Thank You" for what His hands can do for you.

READ PSALM 98:1

The Hands of Jesus

Jesus says, "Look at my hands…"
LUKE 24:39

Again and again, Jesus reached out His hands. He touched people who were sick and made them well. He touched people who were dead, and made them come back to life. He reached out His hand to rescue Peter when Peter was sinking in the sea. He reached out His hands to hug little children (Matthew 19:13-15).

Jesus also stretched out His hands, and let soldiers nail Him to the cross.

Look at your hands, and remember the hands of Jesus. Tell Jesus "Thank You" for what His hands have done for you.

READ AND REMEMBER JOHN 3:35

Safe in God's Hands

Jesus says, "No one can snatch them out of my hand."
JOHN 10:28

Jesus says we are like His sheep, and He is our Shepherd. We listen to His voice. He knows us, and we follow Him. He gives us eternal life. And no one can steal us out of Jesus' hand.

Jesus says that it is God the Father who has given us to Jesus. God is stronger than anyone. No one can steal us out of God the Father's hands.

Jesus says that He and God the Father are One. So praise God that we in Jesus' hands, and in God's hands. And no one can ever steal us away.

READ AND REMEMBER JOHN 10:27-30

Gold Lampstand

God said, "Make a lampstand of pure gold..."
EXODUS 25:31

God told His people to make a beautiful tent and set it up. It was called the Tabernacle. It was a place where God would come and be with His people. God's people could worship Him there. God told them exactly how to make the tent, and how to set it up, and what to put inside it. He told them to put a lampstand inside it. The lampstand had room for seven lights. It was made of pure gold.

The lampstand helped God's people remember that God is our light. Can you give thanks today to the Lord for His light?

READ EXODUS 25:31-40

Seven Lampstands

*In the Bible, John says, "When I turned
I saw seven golden lampstands."*
REVELATION 1:12

One Sunday, the good man John heard a voice behind him. He turned around to see who it was.

John saw seven golden lampstands. And standing with the lampstands was Someone whose face was as bright as the sun. His eyes were like fire. In His right hand were seven stars. His voice was like a waterfall. His words were as sharp and powerful as a sword.

And He said, "I was dead, but look! I am alive forever!"

Yes, this was Jesus. Praise and thank Jesus that He is so bright and mighty.

READ REVELATION 1:9-20

Keep Loving

Jesus says, "The seven lampstands are the seven churches."
REVELATION 1:20

When John saw Jesus standing with the seven golden lampstands, he was afraid. He fell down at Jesus' feet. Jesus reached down and touched him. He told John not to be afraid. And He told John that the seven golden lampstands were for seven churches. Jesus gave messages for John to give to the seven churches.

Jesus gave this message to the first church. He said, "I know how hard you work. But you have forgotten how to love Me. Love Me as you loved Me at first, or else I must take away your lampstand."

Let's not forget to keep showing Jesus our love for Him. How can you do this now?

READ REVELATION 2:1-7

The Gift of Snow

The Bible says, "He spreads the snow like wool
and scatters the frost like ashes."
PSALM 147:16

God makes the snow and sends it down. Snow can come only when He lets it. Every snowy day is a gift from God.

The Bible says that God spreads the snow like wool. Wool is from sheep. Snow can remind us of wool, and wool can remind us of sheep. Sheep can remind us that we are God's sheep, and Jesus is our Shepherd. Just as wool covers the sheep, so the snow covers the earth. In the same way, God's love covers us.

The next time it snows, remember to tell God "Thank You."

READ JOB 37:5-6

Rain and Snow

God says, "As the rain and the snow come down from heaven...
so is my word that goes out from my mouth...."
ISAIAH 55:10-11

When rain and snow come down from the sky, God says this is a picture for us of something else. God sends down rain and snow for a reason. They come down to water the earth, to give it moisture. The crops in our gardens and in the farmers' fields will need this moisture. With this moisture the crops can grow and give us food.

In the same way, God sends down His Word. He sends us His Word for a reason. He gives us His Word to help us grow.

So be glad and praise God. Praise and thank Him that His Word will do what He sends it to do.

READ AND UNDERSTAND ISAIAH 55:6-13

White as Snow

God says, "Though your sins are like scarlet,
they shall be as white as snow."
ISAIAH 1:18

Scarlet is the color red. It is very red, like blood. In God's eyes, our sins were like scarlet. They were blood-red. The wrong things and the bad things we do and say were as red as scarlet.

But God says He can make them as white as snow. How can He do that? He can do it because Jesus died to wash away our sins. Jesus never did anything wrong or bad. Jesus never said anything wrong or bad. He should have never died, and He never had to. He did it only because He loves us.

Praise God today that His Son has died for us to make us as white as snow.

READ PSALM 51:7

Perfume for Jesus

The Bible says, "Perfume and incense bring joy to the heart..."
PROVERBS 27:9

Perfume is what grownups put on anything they want to smell good, including themselves. The Bible speaks three times about women who brought perfume to put on Jesus. Can you remember the three stories?

The first woman had done many bad and ugly things. She came to a house where Jesus was having dinner. She went to Him, and got down beside His feet. She washed His feet with her tears, and dried them with her hair. Then she put perfume on His feet. She loved Jesus because He forgave her for so many bad and ugly things.

Tell Jesus "Thank You" that He can forgive anyone.

REVIEW THE STORY IN LUKE 7:36-50

Perfume for Jesus

The Bible says, "While the king was at his table,
my perfume spread its fragrance."
SONG OF SONGS 1:12

Do you remember the story of the second
woman who put perfume on Jesus? She was
Mary, the sister of Martha and Lazarus.
Jesus was a guest for dinner at someone's
house. Mary was there too. She had
some perfume that cost a lot of money.
She poured it on Jesus' feet. She wiped His
feet with her hair. Everyone in the house
could smell the perfume.

Jesus said Mary was getting His body ready to be buried.
He said that Mary did a beautiful thing. And now, wherever
people tell the good news of Jesus, they also tell about Mary.

What beautiful thing can you do for Jesus?

REVIEW THE STORY IN JOHN 12:1-11

Perfume for Jesus

God said, "Make these into a sacred anointing oil,
a fragrant blend, the work of a perfumer."
EXODUS 30:25

There is one more story in the Bible about women and perfume and Jesus. Do you remember it? After Jesus was killed, some women watched the tomb where two men put the body of Jesus. The women wanted to come back later with spices and perfume to cover Jesus' body. This was how they could show their love for Him.

They went home to get the spices and perfume ready. Then they rested for a day. When they came back to the tomb, Jesus was not there. He was risen from the dead. They never got to put their perfume on His body. But they are happy forever that He is alive. And so are we!

REVIEW THE STORY IN LUKE 23:55-24:8

The Beautiful Pearl

*Jesus says, "The kingdom of heaven
is like a merchant looking for fine pearls."*

MATTHEW 13:45

Jesus talked about a man looking for pearls. The man saw a very beautiful pearl. He went away and sold everything He had, and bought that pearl.

Jesus is like that man looking for pearls. He saw God's people in the world. He knew how beautiful we could be in heaven—as beautiful as a pure, white pearl. Jesus left His heavenly home and came to earth. He gave up everything. He gave up His life. Then He bought God's people. He made us clean and bright, like a pure, white pearl.

Give thanks to Jesus, that He gave up everything He had to make us pure and clean.

LISTEN TO JESUS IN MATTHEW 13:45-46

The Gates of God

The Bible says, "The twelve gates were twelve pearls,
each gate made of a single pearl."

REVELATION 21:21

In the New Jerusalem, each of the twelve gates is a huge pearl.

Come with me, and let's praise God at each gate:

At the first gate: God is holy. *At the second gate:* God is mighty. *The third gate:* God is loving. *The fourth gate:* God is patient. *The fifth gate:* God is fair and just. *The sixth gate:* God is true and never lies. *The seventh gate:* God is good and perfect. *The eighth gate:* God is kind. *The ninth gate:* God is forgiving and merciful. *The tenth gate:* God is beautiful and lovely. *The eleventh gate:* God is wise. *The twelfth gate:* God lives forever.

READ AND ENJOY ROMANS 11:33-36

Families at the Gates

*The Bible says, "On the gates were written
the names of the twelve tribes of Israel."*
REVELATION 21:12

In the New Jerusalem, each of the twelve gates is a pearl. On each gate is written the name of one of the first twelve families in God's people. Look! Here they come through the gates. *At the first gate:* Reuben, strong and mighty. *At the second:* Judah, like a lion. *The third:* Levi, the teachers. *Fourth:* Dan, just and fair. *Fifth:* Joseph, fruitful. *Sixth:* Benjamin, people who are loved. *Seventh:* Simeon, like a sword. *Eighth:* Issachar, people of the mountain. *Ninth:* Zebulun, people by the seashore. *Tenth:* Gad, soldiers. *Eleventh:* Asher, people of rich food. *Twelfth:* Naphtali, like a deer.

Praise God for the families you will one day see in heaven.

EXPLORE GEN. 49; DEUT. 33; EZEK. 48

King's Palaces

In the Bible, David says, "Here I am, living in a palace of cedar..."
2 SAMUEL 7:2

A palace is a big house, fine enough for a king. When God made the good man David king over His people, David had a palace built for himself in Jerusalem. It was built with beautiful cedar logs. The next king was Solomon, David's son. He built an even bigger and finer palace.

But when Jesus came to this world, He never lived in a fine palace. Sometimes He spent the night in other people's houses. Sometimes He slept outside.

Now Jesus is in heaven, which is better than any king's palace on earth. Praise Jesus today that He is our King in the palace of heaven.

LISTEN TO JESUS IN MATTHEW 8:18-20

In Pilate's Palace

The Bible says, "The Jews led Jesus...
to the palace of the Roman governor."
JOHN 18:28

When Jesus lived on earth, a Roman governor named Pilate lived in Jerusalem. He and his soldiers were in charge of Jerusalem. When Jesus was captured by His enemies, they took Him to Pilate's palace. They wanted Pilate to have Jesus killed on the cross.

Pilate asked Jesus, "Are you a king?" Jesus answered that His kingdom is not like other kingdoms. Jesus said His kingdom is the true kingdom. He said everyone who is on the side of truth will listen to Him.

Jesus is the true King. Are you on His side, the side of truth? Do you love to listen to Him?

READ JOHN 18:28-40

In Pilate's Palace

The Bible says, "Pilate went back inside the palace."
JOHN 19:9

At first Pilate did not want to have Jesus killed. After he talked with Jesus in his palace, he went out to speak with the enemies of Jesus. But these enemies still wanted Jesus killed. They shouted, "Crucify! Crucify!"

Pilate went back into his palace. He talked again with Jesus. He told Jesus he could have Jesus killed on the cross. Jesus knew this could only happen because God would let it happen. Jesus was not afraid or worried. Jesus was trusting God.

Jesus' enemies kept shouting, "Crucify Him!" Finally Pilate ordered His soldiers to kill Jesus on a cross. Give thanks to Jesus today that He died on the cross for us.

READ' JOHN 19:1-16

A Bowl with Salt

In the Bible, Elisha said, "Bring me a new bowl,
and put salt in it."
2 KINGS 2:20

The good man Elisha believed in God and obeyed God. So God did mighty miracles through Elisha. Elisha was in a town where the people were unhappy. Their water tasted terrible. And it was not good for the crops they wanted to grow in their gardens and fields. So Elisha said to the people, "Bring me a new bowl, and put salt in it." Elisha went to the place in the ground where their water came from. He poured the salt into the water. Now the water tasted good. And now it was good for crops.

Praise God for the wonderful miracles He can do.

READ THE STORY IN 2 KINGS 2:19-22

Bowls with Prayers

The Bible says, "They were holding golden bowls full of incense,
which are the prayers of the saints."

R E V E L A T I O N   5 : 8

When the good man John looked into heaven, he saw wonderful angels. Four of them were living creatures, each with six wings. He also saw twenty-four older angels. They were dressed in white and wore golden crowns.

John saw all of them fall down and worship Jesus, the Lamb of God. They were holding golden bowls. Inside the golden bowls were the prayers that God's people pray. These prayers could be seen and smelled, like sweet-smelling smoke.

The next time you pray, remember how the prayers of God's people are there in those golden bowls.

REVIEW REVELATION 8:1-4

Bowls of Punishment

The Bible says, "They gave to the seven angels seven golden bowls filled with the wrath of God, who lives for ever and ever."
REVELATION 15:7

Someday God's punishment will come on the earth. Angels will be given seven golden bowls. Inside the bowls is punishment from God. This punishment is only for those who do not believe in God or love Him or obey Him.

God wants people to be sorry for the wrong things they have done. He wants them to stop being bad. He wants to help them be good. He wants them to worship Him. He wants them to learn to love and obey Him. This is always what God wants to do when He punishes people.

Praise God that He always loves the people of the world.

READ REVELATION 15:5-8

God's Banner

God says, "I will lift up my banner to the peoples…"
ISAIAH 49:22

Think about a flag shining in the sunlight and blowing in the breeze. Can you see its bright colors? Can you hear it flapping in the wind?

A banner is a flag. It is a flag that gives us a signal. It tells us something. The Bible says that someday God will lift high a banner. It will be high enough so that people from all over the world will see it. God's banner will tell them that they should come to God and to His people.

The next time you see a flag, think about God. Remember how He calls out for people everywhere to come to Him.

READ ISAIAH 49:22

God's Banner

*The Bible says, "In that day the Root of Jesse
will stand as a banner for the peoples…"*
ISAIAH 11:10

Jesus has many names. One of them is the Root of Jesse. Someday, Jesus the Root of Jesse will be like a banner or a flag. He will signal to all the people of the world. He will tell them they should come to Him. People will hurry to where He is.

In this place they can rest and be safe. It is a bright place, a place of glory. Everyone will love being there with Jesus.

Right now, tell Jesus "Thank You" that you know how wonderful it will be to live with Him, and to stand together with Him like a banner on a mountain.

READ AND ENJOY ISAIAH 11:10-12

Our Banners

In the Bible, God's people say, "We will lift up our banners
in the name of our God."

P S A L M   2 0 : 5

When you are glad about God, and sing about God, and talk to other people about God, it is like waving a flag. You wave your banner high. It blows in the breeze. Its colors shine in the sunlight.

This is what it is like in the army of God. Jesus our King and our Captain is leading us into battle. And he will win the battle.

So we are glad. We praise Him because He is the Winner. We praise Him because He can do whatever He wants to do. We praise and thank Him that we are on His side—the winning side!

READ AND ENJOY PSALM 20:4-8

Two Silver Trumpets

God said to Moses, "Make two trumpets
of hammered silver…"
NUMBERS 10:2

When God's people were crossing the desert, the Lord told Moses to make two silver trumpets. When they sounded, they were signals for God's people. When both trumpets sounded, everyone was to meet together to hear God's instructions. If only one trumpet sounded, just the leaders met together.

The trumpets also sounded when God's people were to move on to a new camp, or when they were to go into battle against His enemies. The trumpets also sounded when God's people were to celebrate a holiday.

Thanks to God! He always tells His people what to do.

READ NUMBERS 10:1-10

Trumpets and Shouts

God said to Joshua, "March around the city…
with all the armed men."
JOSHUA 6:3

When God's people came to the Promised Land, His enemies were already there. They did not want to leave.

God's people came to Jericho. Jericho had a strong, high wall all around it. The gates were shut tight. God's enemies did not want to let His people inside.

God told His people what to do. They marched around those walls. They did this each day for six days. On the seventh day they marched seven times. They blew loud trumpets, and shouted. The walls of Jericho fell down. God's people went inside and took Jericho.

Praise God for the mighty miracles He can do.

READ THE STORY IN JOSHUA 6

The Last Trumpet

*The Bible says, "The Lord himself will come down
from heaven…with the trumpet call of God."*
1 THESSALONIANS 4:16

God signals His people to tell us
what to do and when to do it.
His signals are like a trumpet.
Someday Jesus our King will
come back for His people. When
He comes, we will hear a loud
trumpet sounding. It is the trumpet call of God. We will look
up and see Jesus our King and all His angels with Him.
Suddenly we will be with Jesus, and with everyone who
belongs to Him—everyone who has ever believed in Him
and loved Him. We will all live in new bodies forever.

Praise God for everything that will happen on the day we
hear that trumpet.

READ 1 CORINTHIANS 15:50-59

Our King Forever

The Bible says, "The Lord has established his throne in heaven,
and his kingdom rules over all..."

PSALM 103:19

The Lord God Almighty is on His throne. He is the great King. He has always been on His throne. He will be on His throne forever and ever.

On His throne He decides what is right and fair. He is never unfair to us. He always does what is right. His throne is holy. It belongs only to Him. It is in a place by itself, and no one else can ever be King. From His throne He sends out His love and kindness. He hears His people's prayers, and He answers them from His throne.

Praise God that He is our King, today and forever.

READ AND ENJOY PSALM 93:1-2

King Jesus

In the Bible, John says, "I saw a Lamb...
standing in the center of the throne..."
REVELATION 5:6

Jesus was born in Bethlehem. But He is not a baby anymore. He will never be a baby again.

Jesus came to this world to be killed on a cross. Jesus was born to die. He is the Lamb of God who takes away the sins of the world. Now Jesus is in heaven. He is the Lamb of God who stands in the center of God's throne.

Praise Jesus today that He is King of Kings and Lord of Lords. His kingdom will never end. Tell Him today how much you believe in Him, and how much you love Him, and how glad you are that you belong to Him forever.

REVIEW REVELATION 11:15

Jesus Knows

*The Bible says, "Let us then approach the
throne of grace with confidence…"*
HEBREWS 4:16

Jesus came here to die on the cross and to take away our sins.

He is in heaven now, at the throne of God. But He has
not forgotten us. He remembers and sees us. He knows we
are here. He knows what we need. He knows when we are
weak or tired. He knows when it is hard for us to be good.
He knows everything that is happening to
us, and He understands what it is like.

That is why we can be glad to pray. We
can pray to Him for whatever we need.
We can be sure that He will give us what
we need. Pray to Him now, for what
you really need.

READ AND REMEMBER HEBREWS 4:16

David's Harp

The Bible says, "David would take his harp and play."
1 S A M U E L   1 6 : 2 3

In the Bible, David was a good shepherd,
and a good soldier, and a good king.
He was also good at playing the harp.
With his harp he made beautiful music.
When he was young he played his harp
for King Saul. He played whenever King Saul was
troubled and worried. David's music was beautiful.
It made Saul feel better.

Jesus is our Good Shepherd and our Good King.
He can also make good music for us inside, in our hearts.
When we are troubled or worried, we can think about the
words of Jesus. They will be like music to us. They will make
us feel better.

READ AND ENJOY PSALM 57:7-11

David's Harp

In the Bible, David says, "Awake, harp and lyre!
I will awaken the dawn."
PSALM 108:2

One morning, David played his harp and sang a new song to God. He sang about making the morning come awake. We have his song in the Bible. It is called Psalm 108.

David's heart was strong. David sang to God and loved God with all His heart. He promised to praise God wherever he went. He said God's love reaches all the way up to the sky, and is higher than heaven. David prayed that God's glory would shine all over the world. He also asked for God's help.

What can you tell God in a prayer today?

READ AND ENJOY PSALM 108

Angels with Harps

The Bible says, "Each one had a harp…"

REVELATION 5:8

The good man John saw angels in heaven who were holding harps. They sang a new song to Jesus, the Lamb of God. They praised Jesus that He was good enough to open the scroll. He was good enough, because He had been killed. With His blood He bought people for God from all over the world. He made them to be a kingdom for God. They can serve God forever. They will be like kings and queens.

So be glad, and praise Jesus with the angels. Praise Him for what He has done with His blood.

REVIEW REVELATION 5:8-14

Wise Men's Treasures

The Bible says, "They opened their treasures and presented him with gifts of gold and of incense and of myrrh."
MATTHEW 2:11

When Jesus was still a baby, wise men came to find Him. They brought treasures with them. They followed a star. The star was God's signal to tell the wise men where to find Jesus.

The star stopped over a house in Bethlehem. The wise men went inside. They saw the baby Jesus with Mary, His mother. They bowed down and worshiped Jesus. They opened their treasures and gave them to Jesus.

Was it right for them to bow down and worship Jesus? Was it right for them to give Him gifts? Is it right for you to bow down and worship Him? Is it right for you to give Him gifts?

READ THE STORY IN MATTHEW 2:1-12

Treasures in Heaven

Jesus says, "Store up for yourselves treasures in heaven…"
MATTHEW 6:20

Jesus said we can store up treasures in heaven. We can do this right now. The treasures we store in heaven will be ours to enjoy forever. They will never get old or worn-out or broken. They will never be stolen.

The more treasures we store in heaven, the more we will love heaven. We will want to be in heaven, where our real treasure is.

How can we store up treasures in heaven? Listen to Jesus every day. He will tell you what is right and good to do. He will tell you how to help other people. He will tell you how to show your love to Him. Do what He tells you to do, and you will have treasure in heaven.

LISTEN TO JESUS IN MATTHEW 6:19-21

Hidden in Jesus

The Bible says, "In Christ are hidden all the treasures
of wisdom and knowledge."
COLOSSIANS 2:3

The Bible tells us that there is treasure hidden in Jesus.
Treasures of wisdom and knowledge are hidden in Jesus.
You cannot find these wonderful treasures anywhere else.

Only Jesus can teach us this wisdom and this knowledge.
He has these treasures stored up inside Him. They are His
special secrets. But if we will love Him and listen to Him, He
will tell us these secrets. As we listen every day, He will tell
us more and more.

Will you promise to listen to
Jesus every day? Then listen,
and enjoy His new treasures,
day after day after day.

LISTEN TO JESUS IN MATTHEW 28:18-20

"More desirable than gold...

and sweeter than honey..."

That's what Psalm 19 says about Bible truths—

the same rich truths presented just for kids

in Questar's Gold'n'Honey Books